Lecture Notes in Computer Science

Edited by G. Goos and J. Hartmanis

82

John G. Sanderson

A Relational Theory of Computing

Springer-Verlag
Berlin Heidelberg New York 1980

Author

John G. Sanderson
The University of Adelaide
Department of Computing Science
G.P.O. Box 498
Adelaide
South Australia 5001

AMS Subject Classifications (1980): 68B10, 68C01
CR Subject Classifications (1974): 5.20, 5.24

ISBN 3-540-09987-5 Springer-Verlag Berlin Heidelberg New York
ISBN 0-387-09987-5 Springer-Verlag New York Heidelberg Berlin

Library of Congress Cataloging in Publication Data. Sanderson, John G 1929- A relational theory of computing. (Lecture notes in computer science ; 82) Bibliography: p. Includes index. 1. Electronic digital computers--Programming. 2. Metamathematics. I. Title. II. Series. QA76.6.S262. 001.64'2. 80-14303

Printing and binding: Beltz Offsetdruck, Hemsbach/Bergstr.
2145/3140-543210

ACKNOWLEDGEMENTS

The presentation of subject matter of this book was shaped, over a period of years, in lecture courses given to advanced students at the universities of Adelaide and Oxford. I wish to thank them for their interest, their forebearance, and, especially, for their criticism.

I am grateful to Dr. E.F. Codd for pointing out the relevance of Backus' work, and to Chris Marlin, Roman Orszanski and Andrew Wendelborn who have read the book in draft form and made many valuable comments.

Finally, I wish to express my deep gratitude to my wife Gloria, to whom this book is dedicated, for her support and trust over the years when it seemed that the work might never see the light of day.

CONTENTS

Contents

INTRODUCTION

The idea underlying this book is that a comprehensive theory of computing may be developed based on the mathematics of relations. At present, research in each area of the theory of computation is pursued using whatever mathematical equipment appears most appropriate. While this may be the optimal strategy for one area taken in isolation, it is less than optimal for the field as a whole. Communication and cross-fertilization between different areas are inhibited, and it is harder to get a unified, synthetic grasp of the subject as a whole as long as its practitioners do not talk the same language.

The relevance of relational calculi to computing has long been recognized. In particular, Blikle's use of a relational calculus in [4] to compare three methods of program verification comes close to the approach which is being advocated here, and should be read in conjunction with Section 6.2 below. Nevertheless, there does not appear to have been any previous proposal to use these calculi as the basis for a really comprehensive theory.

Naturally, the specialists in the different areas of computing science would need to be convinced that relational theory provides an adequate alternative to their existing mathematical apparatus. At the present time this is not usually the case, so that it has been necessary to devote the first three chapters of the book to developing relational calculi which are suitable for computational applications. Even so, it is clear that much more work will be needed in this area.

The remainder of the book looks at various applications: two chapters deal with data types, two with questions related to programming, and the last chapter is concerned with metatheory.

To reformulate a major part of the theory of computation in relational terms would clearly be a large undertaking involving many workers and extending over a period of years. A book such as this can barely scratch the surface of such a project. Thus, as a matter of policy, I have not attempted to go into any one area in depth, or to bring the most recent advances into the discussion. Rather, I have tried to show how relational theory might be applicable to a number of different areas. The coverage aims to be representative, but is far from complete. Notable omissions are formal languages and automata (except for a hint in Chapter 6), the theory of approximation, complexity theory, and the theory of relational data bases. (This last does not fit into the plan of the present book, but the connection is obvious, and should be explored.)

The relevance of relations to computing arises from the fact that every computation is characterized by a dyadic relation between the input and output states of the computational system in question, namely the relation which is satisfied by precisely those pairs of states <x,y> for which y is a possible result of the computation when it starts from the state x. I will call this the "input-output relation" of the system.

The system performing the computation need not be a digital computer. For example, it may be a mathematical object such as a Turing machine, a Markov algorithm or a formal theory. When it does involve hardware, it may be a subsystem of the total computer like a multiplier; or it may be some virtual system that comes into existence when a particular program runs on the computer. Or, finally, the computational system may involve, not a complete program running on the computer, but some part of a program - a procedure, statement or instruction, for example. All these systems, and others, are amenable to analysis in terms of input-output relations. Given that relations may be used to describe computations from so many points of view and at so many levels, it is natural to ask whether calculi of relations like those of Tarski [30] may not be useful in developing a theory of computation.

Suppose the "computational system" of the last paragraph is a computer executing a program. Then this program determines the computation, and therefore the input-output relation corresponding to it. This is how the situation is habitually described in computing science, but the description may equally well be turned around the other way. Instead of saying that the relation is determined or defined by the program, we may say that the program is a representation of the relation. This actually corresponds more closely to the reality of the situation since in practice a programmer first attempts to decide what it is he is trying to compute (that is, the relation) and only then undertakes the task of coding it in a particular language (thereby producing an executable representation of the relation).

The point that has just been made has two important consequences which may serve as criteria in developing a relational theory of computation. The first is this: in setting up a calculus of relations for use in computing theory we should take careful note of the structuring operations used in the high level languages. They have not been developed at random, but represent the distillation of a great deal of experience gained by language designers as they attempt to combine expressive power and flexibility with conciseness. Now if certain constructs turn out to be very important in a programming language, we will expect some sort of parallels to them to be important in the calculus of relations which the language represents. In any calculus we are constructing, for example, we will look for equivalents to the selection and iteration constructs. These equivalents will occur as _relational operations_ within the calculus which will combine existing relations to form new relations, just as the statement constructors form new statements from existing statements and predicates. Thus if P is the relation corresponding to a Boolean expression, and A and B are relations corresponding to statements, we will expect to find ways of constructing new relations corresponding to _if_ P _then_ A _else_ B and _while_ P _do_ A. (Throughout this book, the notations P → A/B and P?A will be used for these two relational operations.)

The second criterion is this: when seeking to prove any result in the theory of computation, it is important to decide at the beginning whether one is really dealing with programs or with the underlying relations. To prove a theorem concerning relations in terms of programs might well be like proving the commutativity of multiplication in terms of the decimal notation. The logical structure of number theory would certainly be obscured in such a proof, and it would probably be unnecessarily complicated.

Suppose we are concerned with the relationship between iteration and recursion, for example. In a particular language this might involve proving that

```
while p do a
```

is equivalent to

```
if p then
  begin
    a;
    while p do a
  end
```

where "p" is a Boolean expression and "a" a statement. Any proof of this assertion would be based on the semantic specifications of the language, and would be valid for that language alone. If we carry out our investigation at the level of the relational calculus, on the other hand, we will seek to prove that

$$P?A = P \rightarrow A \cdot (P?A)/I$$

where I is the identity relation and P and A arbitrary relations. Once this has been done, the corresponding result becomes available within any language in which <u>while</u> p <u>do</u> a and <u>if</u> p <u>then</u> a <u>else</u> b correctly implement P?A and P→A/B.

These two criteria play an important but unobtrusive role in the development of our theory. The first one guides us into a choice of relational operations whose properties are interesting for the theory of computation, while the second leads us to postpone the discussion of programs to an unexpectedly late stage in the work - unexpected because it is customary to regard programs as primary subject matter of computing theory, whereas we relegate them to the second-class status of representations.

Before coming to grips with our subject matter, there is a question of terminology that needs to be settled. The problem may be illustrated by the equality relation, usually written x=y. Our understanding of this is that for any pair <x,y> the relation either is or is not satisfied, so that corresponding to the relation there is the dyadic predicate Equals defined by

$$\begin{aligned} \text{Equals}(x, y) &= \text{true if } x=y, \\ &= \text{false otherwise.} \end{aligned}$$

Now consider a computation in which the input and output are connected by the equality relation. Clearly, this must be a null computation, which makes no change in the state, and so is characterized by the identity function. In other words, this one mathematical object, which is commonly viewed as a dyadic relation, is, from our point of view, a monadic function. The difference arises from the fact that, whereas in normal practice we are given x and y and the task is to determine whether they satisfy the condition x=y, in the computational application we are given x and required to find a y satisfying the relation.

In order to avoid confusion, I will use the term <u>relator</u> for a dyadic relation when it is being used to specify the set of possible output states which may arise from a given input state. The relator is therefore a generalized function which is multi-valued in order to allow the possibility of non-determinism, and conversely a monadic function is a relator in which there is at most one output corresponding to each input; we will speak of "applying a relator" in just the same way as we speak of applying a function, and will say that a relator is "not applicable" to an input for which there is no output.

It is worth noticing that as a consequence of what has just been said, every relational calculus contains within itself a calculus of functions, so that it will only be necessary to consider functions separately when determinism is a point at issue.

Chapter 1. THE COMPONENTS OF A RELATIONAL CALCULUS

A relational calculus provides us with a formalism for writing expressions whose values are relators. The basic building blocks of these expressions are relator-valued constants (called primitive relators) and relator-valued variables. These are combined by means of relational operations, which are the analogues of the operations of addition, multiplication and so on in elementary algebra. For example, in the expression P→A·(P?A)/I which occurred in the Introduction, I is a primitive relator and P and A are relator-valued variables, "·" and "?" are dyadic relational operators, while "→" and "/" go together in a triadic operation of the general form P→A/B.

In this chapter we shall look at these and other components of relator expressions in detail. Chapter 2 will be devoted to a discussion of some specific calculi, and in Chapter 3 we shall examine techniques for proving equality and inequality of expressions. Before undertaking any of this work, however, there is a preliminary question that needs to be considered.

In all our discussion so far we have spoken of dyadic relators, which map an input state into an output state. In practice, each of these states will consist of a combination of the values of several variables each of which may be structured in its turn. The decision to bundle these variables together artificially in a single "state" needs to be justified, since the alternative exists of keeping them separate and using polyadic rather than dyadic relators.

There is a well known example of a relational calculus which may be interpreted as using polyadic relators: recursive function theory. This is devoted specifically to the definition of functions on the non-negative integers. Certain "initial functions" (primitive relators in our terminology) are taken as given, namely the zero function Z which satisfies $Z(x)=0$ for all x, the successor function N which satisfies $N(x)=x+1$ for all x, and the projection functions U_i^n which select the i-th out of n arguments: $U_i^n(x_1,\ldots,x_n)=x_i$. In addition, three operations are given which permit functions to be combined to produce new functions. These are called substitution, recursion and minimalization.

As an example of how functions are defined in the theory we may take the definition of multiplication in terms of addition and the initial functions. It is based on two properties of multiplication, $x\cdot 0=0$ and $x(y+1)=xy+x$, and has the form

$$\begin{aligned} \text{Prod}(x,\ 0) &= Z(x) \\ \text{Prod}(x,\ y+1) &= \text{Sum}(\text{Prod}(x,\ y),\ x). \end{aligned}$$

(Here recursion is used in obtaining Prod from Sum and Z. Prod and Sum are relator-valued variables; the value of Sum will have been defined previously by another recursion. A detailed account of the theory may be found, for example, in Chapter 3 of [18].)

Recursive function theory, in its usual formulation, is a polyadic relational calculus, then. However, it can easily be represented as a dyadic calculus by taking the operands as sequences of integers, instead of single integers. If this is done (and in fact we shall do it in Theorem 8.1(1)), Prod would have a sequence of length 2 as input and a sequence of length 1 as output. The fact that all recursive functions have a single integer as their value is one reason for taking integers rather than sequences as operands. Another is that, if sequences were used, it would be necessary to include another operation for sequence building. Now it is already possible to represent sequences, with all the necessary operations, by means of Gödel numbering, so that this addition would be redundant - which in no way recommends it to the pure mathematician. Thus it is clear that the special circumstances of recursive function theory militate against its formulation as a dyadic relator calculus; the polyadic character of the theory has no bearing on the way relational calculi should be formulated for use in the theory of computation.

There are two reasons for limiting a relational calculus to dyadic relators in this context. The first is that by so doing we drastically simplify the notation. Because there is never more than one operand in question, namely the "state of the system", it is often possible to omit all references to it without ambiguity. We shall see, in fact, that any computable function can be specified as a relator expression containing no references to operands.

The second reason is that the structure of our data is a matter of vital interest in computing, and is no less important than the structure of our algorithms. Now in the context of a relational calculus our approach to data structuring will be essentially operational. That is to say, we will view data structures through the construction and decomposition operators used to manipulate them. But once we have these operators at our disposal, anything that can be done in terms of polyadic relators can equally well be done with dyadic relators. For both these reasons, then, it is an advantage to combine all the information into a single state and to use dyadic relators to manipulate the components of this state.

1.1 Defining Specific Relators

A relator A on a set S is a subset of S^2. From now on I shall refer to the set S, or any other set which fills the same role, as the base set.

1. Components of a Relational Calculus

The relator A may be viewed in three ways.

(1) It may be seen as a <u>subset of S^2</u>, as was done a moment ago. Adopting this viewpoint enables us to use set-theoretic notation, writing, for example, $\langle x,y\rangle \in A$ or $A \subseteq B$ or $A = B \cup C$ (where B and C are also relators).

(2) A may be seen as a <u>relation</u>. Thus we may write xAy as the equivalent of $\langle x,y\rangle \in A$, and use the predicate calculus in defining new relations. For example,

$$(\forall x)(\forall y)(xIy \iff x=y)$$

will be used as a definition of the identity relator, I; and in fact this technique is adequate for setting up a complete relational calculus.

(3) When A is viewed as a <u>relator</u>, we are thinking in terms of applying it to an element of the base set S, to get another element as result; thus we verbalize xAy as "application of A to x may yield y". The question of determinism is important from this viewpoint.

1.1(1) <u>Definition</u>. The relator A is <u>deterministic</u> if and only if

$$(\forall x)(\forall y)(\forall z)(xAy \wedge xAz \implies y=z);$$

in this case we may write y=A:x in place of xAy. (The colon notation is taken from Backus [1]. For our purposes it is better to have the explicit application symbol ":", rather than indicating application implicitly as in the conventional notation y=A(x).)

Definition 1.1(1) amounts to saying that A is a function, of course, and we shall use the terms "function" and "deterministic relator" interchangeably.

The remainder of Section 1.1 will be concerned with defining certain specific relators which may be used as primitives in relational calculi. Other potential primitive relators will crop up in Section 1.6.

1.1(2) <u>Definition</u>. The <u>identity relator</u>, I, satisfies

$$(\forall x)(\forall y)(xIy \iff x=y).$$

1.1(3) Definition. The abort relator, Z, satisfies

$$(\forall x)(\forall y)\sim xZy.$$

The identity relator leaves the element to which it is applied unchanged. The abort relator, on the other hand, produces no output state at all; in computing terms we would describe its effect precisely by saying that the program had aborted. In set-theoretic terms, Z is the empty set.

1.1(4) Definition. Corresponding to every element, r, of the base set S there is the constant relator, $\bar{\bar{r}}$, which satisfies

$$(\forall x)(\forall y)(x\bar{\bar{r}}y \iff y=r).$$

For the most part we shall defer discussion of the properties of relators to Chapter 3. However, it will be useful for the purposes of Chapter 2 to know whether a given relator expression is or is not deterministic, so questions of determinism will be discussed as they arise.

1.1(5) Corollary. I, Z and the $\bar{\bar{r}}$ are all deterministic.

We will assume that any base set we are using contains two distinguished elements, t and f, which may be put into correspondence with the truth values true and false. Because the two constant relators $\bar{\bar{t}}$ and $\bar{\bar{f}}$ occur frequently and have a particular importance, we will write them as T and F. Thus, since T and F are deterministic, we may use the alternative notation provided in 1.1(1): T:x=t and F:x=f for all x.

1.2 The Composition of Relators

1.2(1) Definition. The composition, A•B, of relators A and B satisfies

$$(\forall x)(\forall y)(x(A\cdot B)y \iff (\exists z)(xAz \wedge zBy)).$$

The result of applying A•B is the same as the result of applying first A and then B. I have departed from the conventional mathematical notation B∘A because the reversal of the relators makes long relator expressions difficult to read.

The notation used here corresponds to the combination of statements S_1 and S_2 to form $S_1;S_2$ in an Algol-like programming language.

1.2(2) Theorem. The composition of deterministic relators is deterministic.

Proof.

In the definition of composition, for any value of x there can be at most one z satisfying xAz, since A is deterministic, and for this z there can be at most one y satisfying zBy, since B is deterministic. □

The definition which follows shows the effect of repeating the application of a relator a constant number of times.

1.2(3) Definition. We define A^n for non-negative integral n recursively by

$$A^0 = I,$$
$$A^{j+1} = A \cdot A^j.$$

1.2(4) Theorem. If A is deterministic, A^n is also deterministic.

Proof by induction on n. □

1.3 Set-Theoretic Operations

We have already seen that relators can be combined by means of the set-theoretic operators because they are subsets of S^2. In this section we shall consider the computational significance of these operations.

1.3(1) Theorem. For all x and y in S,

(i) $x(A \cup B)y \iff xAy \lor xBy$, and

(ii) $x(A \cap B)y \iff xAy \land xBy$.

Proof (for part (i) only).

$$\begin{aligned} x(A \cup B)y &\iff \langle x,y\rangle \in A \cup B \\ &\iff \langle x,y\rangle \in A \lor \langle x,y\rangle \in B \\ &\iff xAy \lor xBy. \end{aligned}$$ □

An immediate consequence of (i) is that the union of deterministic relators is not in general deterministic; the result of applying $A \cup B$ to x may be either the result of applying A or the result of applying B.

While the union operation has obvious relevance to the situation in concurrent processing where any one of several processors may act on the state to modify it, it is hard to see much practical significance in the intersection operation. $A \cap B$ produces a result y from x only if both A and B produce this result.

1.3(2) Definition. $(\forall x)(\forall y)(xA^*y \Longleftrightarrow (\exists n)(xA^n y))$, where n is a non-negative integer.

In computational terms, this means that xA^*y is satisfied if one can arrive at the result y from x by some number of repeated applications of A. A^* will not normally be deterministic.

1.3(3) Theorem. $(A \subseteq B) \Longleftrightarrow (\forall x)(\forall y)(xAy \Longrightarrow xBy)$.

Proof. Immediate from the definition of $\subseteq$. □

The right hand side of the statement of this theorem means that any result which may be obtained using A can also be obtained using B, but the converse is not necessarily true; for some values of x, B may terminate and yield the result y which is not obtainable from A. $\subseteq$ is not a relational operation; it belongs to the metalanguage used in describing relators.

1.4 Conditional Operations

Following the line of attack suggested in the Introduction, we look for relational operations corresponding to the statement constructors of the high level languages, starting in this section with the constructors which select one out of several statements for execution.

1. Components of a Relational Calculus

The most commonly used conditional constructions are, of course, the two variants of the if statement, if <Boolean expression> then <statement-1> else <statement-2>, and if <Boolean expression> then <statement>. The latter form is a special case of the former in which <statement-2> is null, so this form need not be considered separately.

Corresponding to the Boolean expression we will have a relator P which maps the state of the system into one of the base set values t or f. If the value is t then a relator A (corresponding to <statement-1>) is applied to the state as it was before the application of P; if the value is f a relator B corresponding to <statement-2> is applied. This informal description is formalized in

1.4(1) Definition. For any relators P, A and B, $P \to A/B$ is defined by

$$(\forall x)(\forall y)(x(P \to A/B)y \iff xPt \wedge xAy \vee xPf \wedge xBy).$$

This definition is effectively the same as those given by Backus [1] and (after making allowances for the different representations of the Booleans) by Blikle [4].

It is worth looking at 1.4(1) a little more closely to see how it behaves in exceptional conditions.

(a) The definition makes no allowance for P having side-effects, since A or B is applied to the state x as it was before application of P. To achieve the effect of the statement if b then S_1 else S_2 where b is a Boolean expression with side-effects one would use a relator expression corresponding to the modified program

$$u := b; \underline{\text{if}}\ u\ \underline{\text{then}}\ S_1\ \underline{\text{else}}\ S_2$$

where u is a Boolean variable; the side-effect is moved into the assignment, so that the conditional involves no side-effect. Since this can always be done, there is no point in complicating 1.4(1) to gain the dubious advantage of permitting side-effects.

(b) If application of P to x results in neither t nor f, then P→A/B is not applicable to x - that is to say, the application produces no result.

(c) Since P is a general relator and not just a function, we must also consider the case where application of P to x may yield either t or f, so that xPt and xPf both hold. In this case, P→A/B is non-deterministic, and the result may be either the result of applying A or of applying B (as in the case of $A \cup B$).

(d) Non-determinism of A or B also results in non-determinism of P→A/B.

The following corollary to 1.4(1) sums up the situation when all three relators are deterministic.

1.4(2) <u>Corollary</u>. If P, A and B are deterministic, then P→A/B is also deterministic.

The other important conditional statement constructions, after the if forms, are the case construction and the guarded command version of the conditional popularized by Dijkstra [7]. I will only consider the latter, since a case statement may easily be reduced to this form.

In the statement

$$\underline{\text{if}}\ b_1 \rightarrow S_1 \,\square \cdots \square\, b_n \rightarrow S_n\ \underline{\text{fi}}$$

any one of the statements $S_1, \ldots, S_n$ may be executed for which the corresponding Boolean expression b_j (the guard) evaluates to true. We shall retain Dijkstra's notation in the relational operation.

1.4(3) <u>Definition</u>. For any relators $P_1, \ldots, P_n$ and $A_1, \ldots, A_n$, the relator

$$C = \underline{\text{if}}\ P_1 \rightarrow A_1 \,\square \cdots \square\, P_n \rightarrow A_n\ \underline{\text{fi}}$$

satisfies

$$(\forall x)(\forall y)(xCy \Longleftrightarrow (xP_1t \wedge xA_1y) \vee \ldots \vee (xP_nt \wedge xA_ny)).$$

In this definition C will not in general be deterministic, even if all the P's and A's are. If there is no j for which xP_jt is true, C is not applicable to that value of x.

The relationship between this operation and the P→A/B operation will be discussed in Chapter 3.

1.5 Iteration

In this section we shall derive relational operators corresponding to while b do S, and the do $b_1 \rightarrow S_1 \,[]\, \cdots \,[]\, b_n \rightarrow S_n$ od construct of Dijkstra [7].

If the execution of while b do S terminates, the computational system must pass through a sequence of states $x_0,\ldots,x_m$ such that the Boolean expression b evaluates to true for $x_0,\ldots,x_{m-1}$ and to false for x_m, and each x_{j+1} results from x_j by execution of the statement S. I will call such a sequence a process; the definition in terms of relators is

1.5(1) Definition. A process of A governed by P, for arbitrary relators P and A, is a sequence $x_0,\ldots,x_m$ of elements of the base set such that

(i) $x_jPt \wedge x_jAx_{j+1}$ for $0 \leq j < m$, and

(ii) x_mPf.

1.5(2) Corollary. In any process $x_0,\ldots,x_m$ of A governed by P, $x_0A^jx_j$ holds for all $j \leq m$.

1.5(3) Theorem. If P and A are deterministic there is at most one process of A governed by P starting from any given x_0.

Proof.

Since A is deterministic, 1.5(2) and 1.2(4) imply that each x_j is fully determined by x_0. Thus the only way in which two processes could differ would be in their length; one might stop at x_m, while the other, although identical with it up to x_m, extends beyond to x_n for some $n>m$. However, this is not possible, since termination of the first process would require

x_mPf and continuation of the second, x_mPt, and these cannot both be true if P is deterministic. □

This idea of a process may be used to define the iteration operation for relators. We may say that x(P?A)y holds if and only if there is a process $x_0,\ldots,x_m$ of A governed by P such that $x=x_0$ and $x_m=y$, thus making P?A the relator equivalent to <u>while</u> P <u>do</u> A. However, it turns out to be more convenient to adopt the definition of iteration of Blikle [4], which is adapted to our notation in 1.5(4), and then to show that it corresponds to the definition which was just suggested.

1.5(4) <u>Definition</u>. $P?A = (P \rightarrow A/Z)^* \cdot (P \rightarrow Z/I)$.

Referring to 1.2(1) and 1.3(2), we may construe this as follows: x(P?A)y holds if and only if there is an element z of the base set S and an integer m such that $x(P\rightarrow A/Z)^m z$ and $z(P\rightarrow Z/I)y$. Now $P\rightarrow A/Z$ is applicable to any element u of S only if uPt, and if this holds its effect is the same as applying A. Thus $x(P\rightarrow A/Z)^m z$ will hold if and only if there is a sequence $x_0,\ldots,x_m$ satisfying condition (i) of 1.5(1), such that $x=x_0$ and $x_m=z$. On the other hand, $z(P\rightarrow Z/I)y$ holds if and only if zPf and z=y. Thus we arrive at

1.5(5) <u>Theorem</u>. x(P?A)y holds if and only if there is a process $x_0,\ldots,x_m$ of A governed by P such that $x=x_0$ and $y=x_m$.

1.5(6) <u>Corollary</u>. If P and A are deterministic, then P?A is also deterministic.

<u>Proof</u> follows from 1.5(3). □

Notice that P?A is defined in terms of the conditional $P\rightarrow A/B$, so that, as in the case of the conditional, the possibility of P having side-effects is excluded.

The statement <u>do</u> $b_1\rightarrow S_1 \,[]\, \ldots \,[]\, b_n\rightarrow S_n$ <u>od</u> produces an iteration in which, at each step, any S_j may be applied for which the guard b_j evaluates to true; the iteration terminates when all guards are false. In defining the equivalent relational operation I have again followed Blikle [4]. 1.5(7) is a generalization of 1.5(4), and may be interpreted in much the same way as was done for 1.5(4) in the paragraph which followed that definition.

1.5(7) Definition.
$\underline{do}\ P_1 \to A_1 \,\square \dots \square\, P_n \to A_n\ \underline{od}$
$= (P_1 \to A_1/Z \cup \dots \cup P_n \to A_n/Z)^* \cdot (P_1 \to Z/I \cap \dots \cap P_n \to Z/I)$

1.5(8) Corollary. $P?A = \underline{do}\ P \to A\ \underline{od}$.

1.6 Data Structuring Operations

So far we have not had to make any assumptions about the base set except that it contains the elements t and f. When we come to look at structuring operations the situation is different; we can only manipulate structures if there are structures in the base set to be manipulated.

At first sight this seems to pose a major problem, at least if we want our theory to be applicable to practical, everyday computing. How is one to define a base set that contains the enormous diversity of data structures that occur in practice? Fortunately we do not have to answer this question, for, as we shall see in Chapters 4 and 5, it is possible to set up a reproduction of a calculus which has a given base set within another calculus based on a simpler set. Thus we can exercise a certain amount of freedom in choosing a base set without compromising our chance of applying the theory to more complex structures. Let us list some of the options.

(1) Take as the base set the set of non-negative integers, as is done in recursive function theory. In this case, any set of structures which is to be studied is represented by defining a mapping from the set into the integers.

(2) Take as the base set the set of all binary trees which have terminal elements in some set S of atoms. It is not necessary to include the integers in S since they can be

represented by structures (as is done when we use decimal or binary numerals). Also, we know from experience with LISP that this system is effective in representing more general structures.

(3) Take a general set of trees with terminal elements in S; this base set contains the elements of S, and in addition if $x_1,\ldots,x_n$ are elements of the base set, then the n-tuple $\langle x_1,\ldots,x_n\rangle$ is also an element.

(4) We may choose to take a set containing still more complex structures.

Of these four alternatives, (1) puts quite unnecessary difficulties in the way of studying structures, while (3) has already been dealt with in some detail by Backus [1]. Thus I will adopt alternative (2) here, defining a set W of binary trees with atoms t and f as terminal elements; consideration of (4) will be deferred to Chapter 5.

1.6(1) <u>Postulates for the Set W.</u>

(i) t and f are distinct elements of W.

(ii) If x and y are in W then the pair $\langle x,y\rangle$ is also in W.

(iii) t and f are the only elements in W which are not pairs (that is, t and f are the only <u>atoms</u>).

(iv) If $\langle x_1,x_2\rangle=\langle y_1,y_2\rangle$ then $x_1=y_1$ and $x_2=y_2$.

(v) (The Principle of Structural Induction for W.) If Q is a property which may or may not hold for elements of W, and if (a) t and f have the property Q, and (b) whenever two elements x and y of W have the property Q the pair $\langle x,y\rangle$ also has the property Q, then all the elements of W have the property Q.

All the postulates (i) to (iv) are used explicitly at some point or other in the discussion which follows; (v) is needed, as in Peano's Postulates, to guarantee that W is the minimal set satisfying (i) to (iv). (We will have no occasion to use induction over W for other purposes.)

1. Components of a Relational Calculus

It is clear that a relational calculus having W as its base set will require projection relators which select one or other component of a pair.

1.6(2) <u>Definition</u>. The relators X and Y are defined by

$$\text{(i)}\quad (\forall z)(\forall u)(zXu \iff (\exists v)(z = <u,v>)),$$

$$\text{(ii)}\quad (\forall z)(\forall v)(zYv \iff (\exists u)(z = <u,v>)).$$

When applied to a pair <x,y>, X yields x and Y yields y; neither X nor Y is applicable to an atomic element of W since the condition z=<x,y> is not satisfied for any x and y.

Simple relators like X and Y are of no use when we need to build up structured elements of W from their components. Since a relator has by definition only one input there is no way in which the two components can be specified. What we can do, however, is to make use of a relational operation designed for this purpose.

1.6(3) <u>Definition</u>. If A and B are any relators on W, the relator <A,B> satisfies

$$(\forall z)(\forall w)(z<A,B>w \iff (\exists x)(\exists y)(zAx \wedge zBy \wedge w=<x,y>)).$$

The effect of applying <A,B> is the same as the effect of applying A and B separately, and combining the results in a pair. The use of angle brackets for this relational operation does not lead to ambiguity, since we are never concerned with ordered pairs of relators on W.

<u>Examples</u>.

(i) <I,T>:a = <a,t>

(ii) <T,<F,F>>:a = <t,<f,f>>

(iii) <Y,X>:<a,b> = <b,a>

(iv) <Y•X, <X, Y•Y>>:<a,<b,c>> = <b,<a,c>>

(v) X?Y:<t,<t,<f,f>>> = <f,f>

In example (iv), application of Y•X and Y•Y to <a,<b,c>> yield b and c respectively. In (v) the relator Y will be applied repeatedly to any structure of the form <t,<t,...<f,<...>>...>>

until all the t's are stripped off the front of the structure.

1.6(4) Corollary. If A and B are deterministic, <A,B> is also deterministic.

1.6(5) Theorem. Any relator expression involving only the primitive relators T, F, I, Z, X and Y, and the relational operations of the form A•B, A^n, P→A/B, P?A and <A,B> denotes a deterministic relator.

Proof.

All the relators mentioned are deterministic, and each of the five relational operations maps deterministic relators into deterministic relators. □

1.7 Recursion

In this chapter, so far, we have looked at a variety of relators and relational operators that may be used in constructing relator-valued expressions. The underlying motivation has been to enable us to define a whole class of relators by means of these expressions. However, there is another method of defining relators which should be mentioned here, namely recursion.

An equation, P?A = P→A•(P?A)/I, which has already been used twice as an example, will serve again. Suppose we write Q for P?A in this. Then we have the recursive definition

Q = P→A•Q/I

of Q in terms of P and A. As programming experience would lead us to expect, recursion is a powerful device, but is not without problems. From a theoretical point of view, it requires more sophisticated mathematical treatment than the operations we have been looking at earlier in this chapter.

(1) It is not necessarily possible to define a relator by a single equation like the one shown. Auxiliary relators may be required, resulting in a set of simultaneous equations.

(2) It cannot be assumed, without proof, that a recursive definition does in fact define a fixed point. It is possible that there may be no relator satisfying a definition.

(3) If there is one fixed point, there may well be many, so that we also have to consider the question of deciding which of these is the appropriate one from the point of view of the theory of computation.

I will comment briefly on the first only of these points here, since there will be a detailed discussion of the others in Chapter 3.

Let $E_1(Q_1,\ldots,Q_n),\ldots,E_n(Q_1,\ldots,Q_n)$ be relator-valued expressions involving the relators and relational operations that have been defined in this chapter (and possibly others like them) as well as certain variables; we assume, in particular, that each of the variables $Q_1,\ldots,Q_n$ may appear in any of the expressions. Then the set of equations

$$
\begin{aligned}
Q_1 &= E_1(Q_1,\ldots,Q_n),\\
Q_2 &= E_2(Q_1,\ldots,Q_n),\\
&\cdot\ \cdot\ \cdot\ \cdot\ \cdot\ \cdot\ ,\\
Q_n &= E_n(Q_1,\ldots,Q_n),
\end{aligned}
$$

constitutes a recursive definition of the relators $Q_1,\ldots,Q_n$ in terms of any other variables which may occur in the expressions $E_1,\ldots,E_n$.

Chapter 2. A COMPARISON OF SOME RELATIONAL CALCULI

The set of relators on a base set S is the powerset $\{R|R \subseteq S^2\}$ of S^2; following Blikle, I shall denote this by Rel(S).

A particular relational calculus on S is determined by the choice of primitive relators and relational operations, as well as the decision as to whether recursion is or is not to be allowed; the calculus includes all the expressions which may be constructed from the chosen components. Each of the expressions evaluates to a relator in Rel(S) so that, by setting up the calculus, we are effectively defining a mapping from the set of expressions into Rel(S). Or, to put it another way, the calculus defines a representation of a subset of the relators in Rel(S) by the expressions.

From the point of view of set theory, a particular relator A in Rel(S) is nothing but a subset of S^2, distinguished from other relators only by the truth or falsity of the assertion $\langle x,y\rangle \in A$ for each pair $\langle x,y\rangle$. This point of view, although valuable enough for some purposes, has the effect of abstracting from all the qualitative aspects of the relators. By treating a relator as a set of pairs it very effectively conceals its overall significance. For example, the only way to check that a particular relator is the square function would be to verify that it contains exactly the elements of the infinite set $\{\langle n,n^2\rangle|n \text{ integral}\}$. But it is precisely aspects like this which are important from our point of view; and it is these aspects which may be conveyed by the content and structure of the expressions in a relator calculus.

The extent to which a given calculus conveys these qualitative aspects of relators and makes them intelligible depends crucially on the choice of primitive relators and relational operations. I have already pointed out the parallel between relator calculi and programming languages in the Introduction, where I suggested that we should profit from the accumulated experience of language designers in designing our calculi. However, there are differences as well as similarities between calculi and languages, so that the first criterion of the Introduction should be regarded as no more than a way of establishing a first approximation. As the study proceeds, and we investigate a theory of computation based on relational calculi more deeply for its own sake, we must not be surprised if the calculi develop a character of their own and go their own way, diverging from programming languages to some extent.

In this chapter we shall look first at the work of Blikle, an interesting and elegant system, although incomplete from the point of view of this book. This will be followed by a fairly detailed description of a family of calculi based on the set W of Section 1.6; these might be seen as an extension of Blikle's system, although there is an important difference in the way Boolean values are represented. Finally, Backus' system, described in Section 2.3, will provide a useful contrast to those which precede it.

Many other calculi are possible, of course. I mentioned recursive function theory earlier as an example of a non-dyadic calculus and also the calculus of Tarski [30], although this is rather remote from what we need. Another interesting possibility is a calculus having a reflexive domain (Scott [26, 27]) as a base set. The effect of this is that the set of continuous functions (that is, continuous deterministic relators) is isomorphic with the base set so that the two can be identified.

2. Some Relational Calculi

Every element in the base set can also be a relator, or, for that matter, a relational operation. This allows one to make a drastic reduction in the number of primitive components in the calculus, even down to the level of the lambda calculus, which has only two. It has the compensating disadvantage of requiring a good deal more mathematical sophistication than is needed in our approach.

2.1 Blikle's Algebra of Binary Relations

This is used by Blikle [2] as a mathematical tool for the analysis of computations in terms of the iterative systems of Pawlak [21] and Mazurkiewicz algorithms [17]. He uses it again in [4] to provide a common framework for the comparison of three program verification methods. Elsewhere, it occurs in his work as a particular case in the context of the theory of nets.

Blikle has as primitive relators only I and Z. (I shall retain my own notation throughout.) For relational operations, he has the usual operations of set theory (see Section 1.3 above), as well as composition of relators and power of a relator (Definitions 1.2(1) and 1.2(3)), the star operation of Definition 1.3(2), and an additional transitive closure operation, $A^+ = A \cdot A^*$.

None of these operations makes any assumption about the base set except that it is non-empty and in fact Blikle is able to make his system non-specific as to its base set, at the cost of having no explicit provision for manipulating structured data.

Instead of using the elements t and f to represent true and false, he uses I and Z. Particular logical conditions are represented by subsets of I. To see how this is done, let us look at his implementation of the conditional $P \to A/B$.

In place of the relator P he uses two subsets of I which we shall denote I_P and I_{-P}. They are given, within our notational framework, by

$$I_P = P \rightarrow I/Z = \{\langle x,x \rangle \mid xPt\} \text{ and}$$

$$I_{-P} = P \rightarrow Z/I = \{\langle x,x \rangle \mid xPf\}.$$

In place of $P \rightarrow A/B$ Blikle uses the expression $I_P \cdot A \cup I_{-P} \cdot B$ (which can be constructed within his system, since only composition and union are involved). Consider the effect of applying this to an arbitrary element x of the base set. xI_Pz holds if and only if xPt and z=x; thus $x(I_P \cdot A)y \iff xPt \wedge xAy$. Similarly, $x(I_{-P} \cdot B)y \iff xPf \wedge xBy$, so that the effect of $I_P \cdot A \cup I_{-P} \cdot B$ is precisely the same as $P \rightarrow A/B$.

In place of P?A Blikle has $(I_P \cdot A)^* \cdot I_{-P}$. This is adapted to our notation in Definition 1.5(4), and I have explained, following that definition, how it effectively defines an iteration. Also, there is no difficulty in defining the guarded command versions of iteration and the conditional in this system.

Although Blikle's calculus is well suited for the purpose for which he intended it, it does not follow that it is a suitable vehicle for the development of a full-scale theory of computation. To start with, it contains no facilities for manipulating structured data. This may be made good by including, for example, the relators X and Y and the operation $\langle A,B \rangle$ of Chapter 1 - though not without some loss of generality.

A more serious problem (from our point of view, if not Blikle's) is that his choice of relational operations runs counter to the first criterion of the Introduction; they have little in common with the statement constructors which have evolved in language theory. It is true, as we have seen, that iteration and the conditional may easily be defined within Blikle's system - but according to our argument they should be primary components of expressions, not secondary derivatives.

Another question that may be raised concerns the use of I and Z to represent true and false. After all, the Boolean values are treated as data elements in practice, not as procedures. However this is only one aspect of the question, for the relators I_p and I_{-p}, which are natural extensions of his representation of the Booleans, correspond precisely to the guards of guarded commands, so that the choice may be justified as being valid operationally. In fact, each of the alternatives of using t and f or I and Z has its advantages, and the choice should be made with the intended application in mind.

2.2 The Calculi RW and RW^+

These two calculi, which have W for their base set, will be used extensively in the chapters which follow, so that it will be worth giving a precise syntax for them.

2.2(1) Syntax of RW^+

Expression	e	::= u | u where def{ , def}
Definition	def	::= rec id=u | id=u | id(id{ ,id}) =u
Union	u	::= isn {∪ isn}
Intersection	isn	::= cs {∩ cs}
Construct	cs	::= dj | dj→dj/dj | dj?dj | dj!dj
Disjunction	dj	::= cj {or cj}
Conjunction	cj	::= n {and n}
Negative	n	::= cp | not cp
Composition	cp	::= pwr{ •pwr}
Power	pwr	::= p | p^{int} | p*
Primitive	p	::= T | F | X | Y | I | Z | (u) | <u,u>
		| id | id(u{ ,u}) | if gl fi | do gl od
Guarded list	gl	::= dj→dj { ▯ dj→dj}

In these formulae, {s} denotes 0 or more occurrences of the string s, id denotes an identifier and int a non-negative integer constant. An identifier will be a capital letter followed by 0 or more letters or digits.

2. Some Relational Calculi

The features of RW^+ which have not been defined in Chapter 1 are the "Boolean" operations and, or and not and the relational operation of the form A!P. These may be regarded as purely notational extensions, since they may be defined in terms of the other operations in the calculus:

2.2(2) Definition. For any relators P and Q

(i) not P = P→F/T

(ii) P and Q = P→Q/F

(iii) P or Q = P→T/Q

2.2(3) Definition. A!P = A·(not P ? A).

Notice, in these definitions, that and and or are not commutative. For example, if P and Q are functions and P:x = f but Q:x is undefined, then (P and Q):x = f whereas (Q and P):x is undefined.

A!P corresponds to the programming language construct, repeat A until P.

The syntax of RW^+ does not allow for the nesting of definitions or for parameters in recursive definitions. All definitions which are recursive or form part of a cycle of recursive definitions are to be marked rec; those not marked rec are effectively abbreviations, so that it will be possible to eliminate them by a finite number of substitutions. These rather limited definitional facilities are sufficient for everything we need to do with RW^+.

There is a network of equivalences (which will be discussed in Chapter 3) which makes it possible to eliminate several components without reducing the set of relators represented by the calculus. For example, I and Z are redundant since I=F?T and Z=T?T; union is redundant since $A \cup B$ = if T→A ▯ T→B fi; and, of course, all those components like and and or which are defined in terms of other components are redundant if the components used in their definitions are included.

2. Some Relational Calculi

Because it includes the union and *if fi* operations, RW^+ defines non-deterministic as well as deterministic relators (functions). An important class of sub-calculi of RW^+ comprises the calculi which define only functions - important because most of the computing done in practice is concerned with the evaluation of functions.

According to Theorem 1.6(5), any relator expression involving only T, F, X, Y, I and Z and the relational operation of the form A•B, A^n, P→A/B, P?A and <A,B> denotes a function. As in RW^+, however, some of these components are redundant; clauses (i) and (ii) in the following definition specify a minimal set.

2.2(4) *Definition*. The calculus RW includes only those expressions of RW^+ which may be formed using

(i) the primitive relators T, F, X and Y,

(ii) the relational operations of the form A•B, P→A/B, P?A and <A,B>,

(iii) non-recursive definitions, and

(iv) other components of RW^+ which can be shown to be purely notational extensions of the components provided for in (i), (ii) and (iii).

It is clear that only deterministic relators can be defined by expressions in RW.

It may seem anomalous to include P?A in (ii) while excluding A*, since P?A is defined in terms of A* in 1.5(4). However, P?A can be defined from first principles by virtue of 1.5(5), and the equation A* = (T ∪ F)?A may be used to define A* in terms of P?A, so that P?A and A* have equal claims to the title of the "primitive iterative operation".

Clauses (iii) and (iv) in the definition may also seem a trifle strange, in that what has just been removed with one hand by (i) and (ii) is put back by (iii) and (iv) with the other. The reason for formulating the definition in this way is this:

when we come to discuss computability we will need to express RW in terms of one of the existing systems which defines the computable functions, and for this purpose it is desirable that RW be as compact as possible; on the other hand, we also use RW in much the same way as one uses a programming language for defining functions, so that it needs to be as powerful as possible. Now the purely notational extensions of (iii) and (iv) do not increase the range of functions which can be defined, they merely allow us to write definitions more briefly, so that when we need to express RW in terms of another system it will be sufficient to do it for (i) and (ii) alone.

The effect of (iv) is to permit the use of I, Z and the forms A!P, _not_ P, P _and_ Q, P _or_ Q and A^n. We shall see in a moment that guarded commands may also be used in some circumstances.

2.2(5) _Theorem_. If the P_j are all functions, and for each x in S there exists an i, $1 \leq i \leq n$, such that the P_j satisfy the conditions

$$P_j{:}x = t \text{ when } j = i, \text{ and}$$
$$P_j{:}x = f \text{ when } j \neq i,\ 1 \leq j \leq n,$$

then

$$\underline{\text{if}}\ P_1 \rightarrow A_1 \,\square \cdots \square\, P_n \rightarrow A_n\ \underline{\text{fi}} =$$
$$P_1 \rightarrow A_1/(P_2 \rightarrow A_2/(\ldots(P_n \rightarrow A_n/Z)\ldots)).$$

Proof. Expand the right hand side using definition 1.4(1).

$$x(P_1 \rightarrow A_1/(\ldots(P_n \rightarrow A_n/Z)\ldots))y$$
$$\Longleftrightarrow xP_1t \wedge xA_1y$$
$$\vee\ xP_1f \wedge xP_2t \wedge xA_2y$$
$$\vee\ xP_1f \wedge xP_2f \wedge xP_3t \wedge xA_3y$$
$$\cdot \quad \cdot \quad \cdot \quad \cdot \quad \cdot \quad \cdot \quad \cdot \quad \cdot$$
$$\vee\ xP_1f \wedge \ldots \wedge xP_{n-1}f \wedge xP_nt \wedge xA_ny.$$

Since xP_jt holds for exactly the one value i of j and xP_jf for all the others, we see that

$$xP_1f \wedge xP_2f \wedge \ldots \wedge xP_jt$$

is true if and only if j = i, so that this conjunction could equally well be written simply as xP_jt. Thus we may drop the terms of the form xP_jf from the beginning of each line of the expansion, which leaves us with the definition of <u>if</u> $P_1 \rightarrow A_1 \,[\!]\, \ldots \,[\!]\, P_n \rightarrow A_n$ <u>fi</u> given in 1.4(3). □

This theorem means that we may use the guarded command form of the conditional in RW in any case where the conditions of the theorem are satisfied. Theorem 3.3(8) will show that similar conditions also hold for the <u>do</u> <u>od</u> operation. We may sum this up as follows:

2.2(6) <u>Corollary</u>. The guarded command forms of iteration and the conditional may be used in RW when the guards are mutually exclusive total predicates.

2.3 Backus' Functional Programming System

This system was described by Backus in the 1977 ACM Turing Award Lecture, and the paper [1] which followed it. His concern is to provide an effective alternative to what he calls the von Neumann languages, that is to say, to the great majority of contemporary languages which constrain their users to think in terms of word-at-a-time operations on variables. He did not write his paper with the intention of defining a relational calculus (or rather, a functional calculus - he has no non-deterministic relators). In fact, he makes no distinction between a calculus and a programming language. Nevertheless, the FP (functional programming) system which he describes in Section 11 of his paper is a functional calculus, while the FFP (formal functional programming) system of Section 13 is a programming language proper, since it involves the representation of functions by elements of the base set.

The fact that Backus uses a functional rather than a relational calculus allows us to make an interesting comparison between the two. He finds it necessary to include an "undefined" element, "bottom", in his base set ("set of objects" in his terminology), and in almost every definition of Section 11 there is an explicit provision for the possibility that a result may be undefined. This all adds up to a significant complication of the whole system, and presents a striking contrast with the definition of a relational calculus, in which there is no need to mention undefined results.

The reason for this difference is easy to see. When applying a function, the normal situation is that it should produce exactly one result. The case where it produces no result is an exception, and must be treated separately. But when a relator is applied to an operand there is no expectation as to the number of results. Any number may be produced, including none at all, so that the notation takes account of an application being undefined without having to make special provision for it. Thus we see that there is an advantage in using relators rather than functions, even when all the relators used happen to be functions and we are dealing with a purely deterministic system.

When discussing RW I pointed out a reason for adopting a minimal set of primitive relators and relational operations: it is necessary to implement RW within (in fact) the lambda calculus in order to prove that it defines only computable functions, so that any redundancy in RW adds to the labour of this implementation. There is another reason connected with the theory of data types. When we set up a new data type in a programming language we provide, among other things, representations of the objects in the new type and implementations of the functions on these objects. The fact that there are no numbers in RW, nor any structures more complex than pairs, gives us the opportunity to study this kind of process within the calculus for data types like the integers and arrays which are simple and well understood. It is pragmatic reasons like these which lead us to use RW extensively for examples in this book. The question of whether one calculus is better than another is decided by the intended application.

Backus selects his primitives on equally pragmatic grounds. He wishes to demonstrate the existence of a viable alternative to the von Neumann languages, so that he needs to be able to produce solutions to significant programming problems without troubling about deriving his primitive relators from a minimal set. Thus he chooses a system having a high degree of redundancy.

This manifests itself first of all in the base set, where he allows n-tuples of arbitrary finite length. To be able to manipulate these with ease he needs a fairly extensive set of primitive relators (functions). Also, he takes the normal logical and arithmetic operators for granted.

The area in which Backus is most likely to achieve his objective of bypassing the "von Neumann bottleneck" is in string and array processing. He includes two relational operations specifically for this purpose in addition to the four basic operations of RW. These are his "insert", which transforms a dyadic function like Sum into the corresponding continued operation (sigma) and "apply-to-all" which applies a monadic function to all the elements of an array to produce another array. It is interesting to see how he can combine his primitives by means of these operations to express various algorithms in a terse, variable-free form.

The final comparison I wish to make concerns his primitive functions "atom" and "eq"; let us look in particular at eq, which tests for equality. This is not present in RW, but in this case it is not a matter of Backus' system being redundant. It appears that there is, in fact, no way in RW of testing for equality of arbitrary elements of W. Does this mean that RW is incomplete?

2. Some Relational Calculi

To answer this question, I shall anticipate very briefly some of the developments of Chapter 4. We shall find there that, although we do not have an equality test which is applicable to arbitrary elements of W, we can develop tests applicable to particular subsets. For example, when we define a set of numerals within W representing the non-negative integers, we will be able to test for equality of two numerals. The trick, then, is to use a representation of any set in which we are interested which allows testing of equality - and the curious thing which comes out of this is that we can set up a representation of W within W which does have an equality test.

Chapter 3. PROPERTIES OF RELATORS

One of the objectives in setting up relator calculi like those of Chapter 2 is to enable us to represent relators by expressions; the way we have done this ensures that the relator represented by each expression is precisely and unambiguously defined. A second objective, which will occupy us in this chapter, is to elaborate an algebra of relators. We may want to use this to decide whether two expressions denote the same relator, or again, whether one denotes a relator which is a subset of the other. In Chapter 6 we shall see how these algebraic results may be used to prove equivalence of programs.

If we look back over the definitions of primitive relators and relational operations of the last two chapters, we find that two distinct styles occur. One has the general form

$$(\forall x)(\forall y)(xEy \iff P(x,y))$$

where E is the relator or expression to be defined, and P is a predicate in x and y; the definition of A•B in 1.2(1) is typical. In the other style, E is simply defined in terms of previously defined components, without the base set elements x and y being invoked. Definition 2.2(2)(ii), P <u>and</u> Q = P→Q/F, is an example of this. I shall call the former a "definition from first principles" and the latter an "algebraic definition".

We shall find that the same distinction occurs in proving equality (or inequality) of expressions. In many cases we shall have to use a first principles proof which involves showing that

$$(\forall x)(\forall y)(xE_1y \iff xE_2y)$$

to prove that $E_1 = E_2$. In other cases, we will be able to obtain a proof by algebraic manipulation, using known first principles theorems in the process - a notable example of this is Theorem 3.3(6). (The parallel with elementary differential calculus is not fortuitous. It results from the fact that in both cases we have a system with semantics specified in terms of another, external system.)

Wadge [32] has developed a natural deduction system for relational calculi which is essentially the same as our first principles method. For our present purpose, however, I believe it is better to use the predicate calculus, since it is well known, and is used in a quite straightforward way whenever it occurs. A list of relevant formulae involving quantifiers is given in an appendix. References to these formulae occurring in proofs will be prefixed by the letter A. Throughout Chapter 3, formulae involving x and y will be taken to be prefixed by the universal quantifiers $(\forall x)(\forall y)$.

Sections 3.1 to 3.4 follow roughly the same order as was used in Chapter 1 in dealing with the relational operations. Proofs which are routine have often been omitted.

Although the notation of RW^+ has been used throughout this chapter, many of the properties discussed apply to a wide range of calculi. For example, in Section 3.1, the only assumption that is made about the base set is that it is non-empty, so that results proved there can be used in any calculus for which they are relevant. Similarly, Sections 3.2 and 3.3 stipulate only that the base set contains the elements t and f, so that results from these sections apply to a system like Backus'.

Section 3.5 is different in character from the preceding sections. It is concerned with the existence and uniqueness of relators which are defined recursively, rather than with their properties, which have been studied extensively by other authors (see for example, [3, 19, 20, 29]).

3. Properties of Relators

3.1 Composition and Set-theoretic Operations

The only assumption made in proving results in this section is that the base set is non-empty. A, B and C stand for arbitrary relators. Many of the results given here will be found in [4].

3.1(1) Theorem.

(i) $A \cdot I = I \cdot A = A$

(ii) $A \cdot Z = Z \cdot A = Z$

The behaviour of I and Z shown here is exactly what one would expect intuitively from their correspondence with the null and abort statements in programming languages. The theorem which follows is the first example of a proof involving the rules for quantifier manipulation given in the appendix. It is by virtue of this theorem that we are able to omit parentheses from sequences of compositions.

3.1(2) Theorem. $A \cdot (B \cdot C) = (A \cdot B) \cdot C$.

Proof.

$x(A \cdot (B \cdot C))y$

$\Leftrightarrow (\exists z)(xAz \wedge z(B \cdot C)y)$	by 1.2(1)
$\Leftrightarrow (\exists z)(xAz \wedge (\exists w)(zBw \wedge wCy))$	by 1.2(1)
$\Leftrightarrow (\exists z)(\exists w)(xAz \wedge zBw \wedge wCy)$	by A2
$\Leftrightarrow (\exists w)(\exists z)(xAz \wedge zBw \wedge wCy)$	by A6
$\Leftrightarrow (\exists w)((\exists z)(xAz \wedge zBw) \wedge wCy)$	by A2
$\Leftrightarrow (\exists w)(x(A \cdot B)w \wedge wCy)$	by 1.2(1)
$\Leftrightarrow x((A \cdot B) \cdot C)y$	□

3.1(3) Corollary. $A \cdot A^n = A^n \cdot A$.

A* is the non-deterministic relator derived from A by allowing it to be applied any number of times (zero or more). Part (i) of the next theorem unrolls the loop; the I corresponds to 0 applications of A, and $A \cdot A^*$ to 1 or more. In 3.1(5), $Z^* = I$ because $Z^0 = I$ by 1.2(3).

3. Properties of Relators

3.1(4) Theorem.

(i) $A^* = I \cup A \cdot A^*$

(ii) $A \cdot A^* = A^* \cdot A$

Proof (of part (i) only).

$x(I \cup A \cdot A^*)y$

$\iff xIy \lor (\exists z)(xAz \land zA^*y)$ by 1.2(1), 1.3(1)

$\iff xIy \lor (\exists z)(\exists n)(xAz \land zA^ny)$ by 1.3(2), A2

$\iff xIy \lor (\exists n)(\exists z)(xAz \land zA^ny)$ by A6

$\iff xA^0y \lor (\exists n)(xA^{n+1}y)$ by 1.2(3)

$\iff xA^*y$

where n is a non-negative integer. □

3.1(5) Theorem. $I^* = Z^* = I$.

3.1(6) Theorem.

(i) $A \cdot (B \cup C) = A \cdot B \cup A \cdot C$

(ii) $(B \cup C) \cdot A = B \cdot A \cup C \cdot A$

(iii) $A \cdot (B \cap C) \subseteq A \cdot B \cap A \cdot C$

(iv) $(B \cap C) \cdot A \subseteq B \cdot A \cap C \cdot A$

Proof (for part (iii) only).

$x(A \cdot (B \cap C))y$

$\iff (\exists z)(xAz \land z(B \cap C)y)$ by 1.2(1)

$\iff (\exists z)(xAz \land zBy \land zCy)$ by 1.3(1)(ii)

$\iff (\exists z)((xAz \land zBy) \land (xAz \land zCy))$

$\implies (\exists z)(xAz \land zBy) \land (\exists z)(xAz \land zCy)$ by A5

$\iff x(A \cdot B)y \land x(A \cdot C)y$ by 1.2(1)

$\iff x(A \cdot B \cap A \cdot C)y$ by 1.3(1)(ii)

Notice that when proving parts (i) and (ii) we will have an equivalence instead of an implication in the fifth line, so that equality always holds. □

If $A \subseteq B$ then any result obtainable by application of A can also be obtained by applying B, but B may give results which are not given by A. The next theorem shows how this ordering of relators interacts with composition and its derivatives. In fact, parts (i) and (ii) of this theorem are equivalent to saying that composition, regarded as a function on relators, is monotonic. In Theorem 3.5(2) we shall see that all the relational operations of RW^+ are continuous functions, which implies that they are monotonic, so that similar properties to those of 3.1(7) hold for all the operations. For example, if $A \subseteq B$, then $\langle A,C\rangle \subseteq \langle B,C\rangle$ and $P?A \subseteq P?B$. (3.1(7) is included here because it is required in 3.3(1).)

3.1(7) Theorem. If $A \subseteq B$ then

$$\text{(i)} \quad A \cdot C \subseteq B \cdot C$$

$$\text{(ii)} \quad C \cdot A \subseteq C \cdot B$$

$$\text{(iii)} \quad A^n \subseteq B^n$$

$$\text{(iv)} \quad A^* \subseteq B^*$$

3.2 Conditional Operations and their Derivatives

It is assumed in this section that the base set contains the elements t and f.

3.2(1) Theorem.

(i) $T \rightarrow A/B = A$

(ii) $F \rightarrow A/B = B$

In practice, this theorem is equivalent to saying that if b is constant in a statement such as if b then S_1 else S_2, this statement can be replaced by S_1 or S_2, depending on whether b has the value true or false. The next theorem provides a justification for the practice of compiler writers who effectively translate Boolean expressions in an if statement into nested if statements - but notice also that and and or are not precise equivalents of the Boolean operations of the same name (see the comment after 2.2(3)). This theorem is exact, but the optimizing device used by the compiler writers is not.

3.2(2) Theorem.

(i) (not P)$\rightarrow$A/B = P$\rightarrow$B/A

(ii) (P and Q)$\rightarrow$A/B = P$\rightarrow$(Q$\rightarrow$A/B)/B

(iii) (P or Q)$\rightarrow$A/B = P$\rightarrow$A/(Q$\rightarrow$A/B)

Proof (for part (iii) only).

x((P$\rightarrow$T/Q)$\rightarrow$A/B)y

$\iff$ x(P$\rightarrow$T/Q)t$\wedge$xAy $\vee$ x(P$\rightarrow$T/Q)f$\wedge$xBy by 1.4(1)

$\iff$ (xPt$\vee$xPf$\wedge$xQt)$\wedge$xAy $\vee$ xPf$\wedge$xQf$\wedge$xBy

$\iff$ xPt$\wedge$xAy $\vee$ xPf$\wedge$(xQt$\wedge$xAy $\vee$ xQf$\wedge$xBy)

$\iff$ x(P$\rightarrow$A/(Q$\rightarrow$A/B))y □

Lemma 3.3(9) may also be noted here. This is one of a family of results concerning the nesting of conditionals which are very easily proved.

We next seek to throw a little more light on the not, and and or operations. Notice that we use the term "predicate" by analogy in 3.2(3); the sense is not precisely the same as in logic, since the results of application are t and f rather than true and false.

3.2(3) Definition. A function P is a predicate if whenever P:x=y holds, y is either t or f.

For the purposes of the next theorem we set up a Boolean algebra on the elements t and f of the base set. The connectives will be written NOT, AND, OR and so on. For example, x AND y has the value t if both x and y are t, the value f if either or both are f, and is undefined if either x or y is not in the set {t,f}. (This notation is local to Theorem 3.2(4) and must not be confused with the notation of Section 5.3.)

3.2(4) Theorem. If P and Q are predicates, and P:x and Q:x are defined for the value of x in question, then

(i) (not P):x = NOT (P:x)

(ii) (P and Q):x = (P:x) AND (Q:x)

(iii) (P or Q):x = (P:x) OR (Q:x)

Proof.

Check the truth tables, noting that if P, Q and R are predicates defined for x,

$$(P \rightarrow Q/R):x = Q:x \text{ if } P:x=t$$
$$= R:x \text{ if } P:x=f. \qquad \square$$

It follows from this that if P and Q are total predicates, then not, and and or obey the usual laws of Boolean algebra - associativity, commutativity, distribution, De Morgan's laws and so on. The failure of commutativity cited after 2.2(3) is only possible because in that case Q is not a total predicate.

From the mathematical point of view, the next two theorems relate to the distribution of composition with respect to the conditional. In practical programming they provide a useful way of reducing the size of a program by removing common statements from the two branches of a conditional (as well as the condition in 3.2(6)). Similar results may easily be derived for guarded commands from the conditional using 3.2(7) with 3.1(6).

3.2(5) Theorem. $(P \rightarrow A/B) \cdot C = P \rightarrow A \cdot C/B \cdot C$

Proof.

$x((P \rightarrow A/B) \cdot C)y$

$\Leftrightarrow (\exists z)(x(P \rightarrow A/B)z \wedge zCy)$

$\Leftrightarrow (\exists z)((xPt \wedge xAz \vee xPf \wedge xBz) \wedge zCy)$

$\Leftrightarrow (\exists z)((xPt \wedge xAz \wedge zCy) \vee (xPf \wedge xBz \wedge zCy))$

$\Leftrightarrow (\exists z)(xPt \wedge xAz \wedge zCy) \vee (\exists z)(xPf \wedge xBz \wedge zCy)$ by A5

$\Leftrightarrow xPt \wedge (\exists z)(xAz \wedge zCy) \vee xPf \wedge (\exists z)(xBz \wedge zCy)$ by A2

$\Leftrightarrow x(P \rightarrow A \cdot C/B \cdot C)y$ $\square$

3.2(6) Theorem. $A \cdot (P \rightarrow B/C) \subseteq A \cdot P \rightarrow A \cdot B/A \cdot C$, with equality holding if A is deterministic.

Proof.

$x(A \cdot (P \rightarrow B/C))y$

$\Leftrightarrow (\exists z)(xAz \wedge (zPt \wedge zBy \vee zPf \wedge zCy))$

$$\iff (\exists z)(((xAz \wedge zPt) \wedge (xAz \wedge zBy) \vee ((xAz \wedge zPf) \wedge (xAz \wedge zCy)))$$
$$\iff (\exists z)((xAz \wedge zPt) \wedge (xAz \wedge zBy))$$
$$\qquad \vee (\exists z)((xAz \wedge zPf) \wedge (xAz \wedge zCy)) \qquad \text{by A5}$$
$$\implies (\exists z)(xAz \wedge zPt) \wedge (\exists z)(xAz \wedge zBy)$$
$$\qquad \vee (\exists z)(xAz \wedge zPf) \wedge (\exists z)(xAz \wedge zCy) \qquad \text{by A5}$$
$$\iff x(A \cdot P \to A \cdot B / A \cdot C)y$$

To see that equality holds if A is deterministic, we need to understand why the fifth line is only an implication, and not an equivalence.

Consider the formula

$$(\exists z)(M(z) \wedge N(z)) \implies (\exists z)M(z) \wedge (\exists z)N(z).$$

If there are some values of z which make both M(z) and N(z) true, then any of these values will make them true separately, so that the implication follows. But on the other hand, the fact that some z make M(z) true, and some other z make N(z) true, does not imply the existence of any one z which makes them simultaneously true. If we look at the line containing the implication in the proof above we see that in each of the four cases, z must satisfy xAz. But if A is deterministic there is at most one z which satisfies this for any x, so that we can bring the whole expression within the scope of a single quantifier, $(\exists z)$, without changing its value.

The following example (due to Duncan McCaskill) shows that equality does not always hold. Let $M = T \cup F$. Then application of $M \cdot (I \to F/I)$ to any x yields f, whereas application of $M \cdot I \to M \cdot F / M \cdot I = M \to F/M$ may yield either t or f. □

We next see how the simple conditional, P→A/B, and the guarded command form are related. The most important difference is that the guarded command conditional can give a non-deterministic result from deterministic operands, unlike the simple conditional. This is indicated by the presence of the union operations in 3.2(7). On the other hand, P→A/B is not just a special case of the guarded command form, since <u>not</u> cannot be expressed as a pure guarded command conditional. (Theorem 2.2(5) is also relevant in the present context.)

3.2(7) Theorem.

$$\underline{\text{if}}\ P_1 \rightarrow A_1 \,\square\, \ldots \,\square\, P_n \rightarrow A_n\ \underline{\text{fi}} = P_1 \rightarrow A_1/Z \cup \ldots \cup P_n \rightarrow A_n/Z$$

Proof follows from 1.4(3), 1.4(1) and 1.3(1). □

3.2(8) Theorem.

$$P \rightarrow A/B = \underline{\text{if}}\ P \rightarrow A\ \square\ \underline{\text{not}}\ P \rightarrow B\ \underline{\text{fi}}$$

Proof.

$x(\underline{\text{if}}\ P \rightarrow A\ \square\ \underline{\text{not}}\ P \rightarrow B\ \underline{\text{fi}})y$

$\iff xPt \wedge xAy \vee x(P \rightarrow F/T)t \wedge xBy$

$\iff xPt \wedge xAy \vee xPf \wedge xBy$

$\iff x(P \rightarrow A/B)y$ □

Notice that if we wished to use the if fi construct as the basic conditional relational operation in setting up a relator calculus, we could redefine not to be independent of the $P \rightarrow A/B$ construct:

$$x(\underline{\text{not}}\ P)y \iff xPt \wedge y=f \vee xPf \wedge y=t.$$

3.2(9) Corollary.

(i) $P \rightarrow A/Z = \underline{\text{if}}\ P \rightarrow A\ \underline{\text{fi}} \subseteq A$

(ii) $P \rightarrow Z/B = \underline{\text{if}}\ \underline{\text{not}}\ P \rightarrow B\ \underline{\text{fi}} \subseteq B$

(iii) $P \rightarrow A/B = P \rightarrow A/Z \cup P \rightarrow Z/B \subseteq A \cup B$

(iv) $\underline{\text{if}}\ P_1 \rightarrow A_1 \,\square\, \ldots \,\square\, P_n \rightarrow A_n\ \underline{\text{fi}} \subseteq A_1 \cup \ldots \cup A_n$

3.3 Iteration Operations

In this section, as in 3.2, the only assumption made is that the base set contains t and f.

3.3(1) Theorem. $P?A \subseteq (P \rightarrow A/Z)^* \subseteq A^*$

Proof.

We have $P \rightarrow Z/I \subseteq I$ from 3.2(9), so that

$P?A = (P \rightarrow A/Z)^* \cdot (P \rightarrow Z/I)$ by Def. 1.5(4)

$\subseteq (P \rightarrow A/Z)^* \cdot I$ by 3.1(7)

$= (P \rightarrow A/Z)^*$ by 3.1(1)

which proves the first part. Also, from 3.2(9), $P \rightarrow A/Z \subseteq A$, so that the second part follows from 3.1(7). □

3. Properties of Relators

The next theorem plays an important part in the axiomatic approach to the correctness of programs. It is incorporated in Hoare's rule giving the semantics of the while statement [11, 12], and is equally essential to the more recent techniques which aim at enabling the programmer to write a correct program in the first place, rather than proving it correct after it has been written. Corollary 3.3(3) has been included here because it will be needed when we come to look at computability.

3.3(2) Theorem. $x(P?A)y \Longrightarrow yPf$

Proof.

From 1.5(4) and 1.2(1) we have

$$x(P?A)y \iff (\exists z)(x(P\rightarrow A/Z)^*z \wedge z(P\rightarrow Z/I)y).$$

However, $z(P\rightarrow Z/I)y$ implies $y=z$ and zPf. □

3.3(3) Corollary. $(\exists y)(x(P?I)y) \iff xPf$

Proof.

From 3.3(1), $P?I \subseteq I$ so that $x(P?I)y$ implies $x=y$; but yPf from the theorem, so that the left hand side implies the right. The reverse implication is immediate from 1.5(4). □

Suppose we have a process which passes through a series of states from x_0 terminating in x_n. Then it should be possible to re-start it in any one of the intermediate states and have the remainder of the process repeat (at least if it is deterministic - if it is non-deterministic, the former process will provide a possible sequence of states for the new one). The next theorem formalizes this intuitive understanding.

3.3(4) Theorem. Let $x_0,\ldots,x_n$ be a process of A governed by P. Then $x_i(P?A)x_n$ for all i, $0 \leq i \leq n$.

Proof.

If $x_0,\ldots,x_n$ is a process of A governed by P, then conditions (i) and (ii) of 1.5(1) imply that any subsequence $x_i,\ldots,x_n$ is also one. The theorem follows from 1.5(5). □

3.3(5) Theorem. For all A,

$$\text{(i) } F?A = I$$

$$\text{(ii) } T?A = Z$$

Proof.

For part (i):

$F?A = (F \rightarrow A/Z)^* \cdot (F \rightarrow Z/I)$ by 1.5(4)

$= Z^* \cdot I$ by 3.2(1)

$= I$ by 3.1(5)

For part (ii), notice that x(T?A)y would imply yTf by 3.3(2). □

The two results just proved correspond to the fact that the statements while false do S and while true do S are respectively null and non-terminating. They are useful in RW in that they enable us to define I and Z in terms of T and F using the iteration operation.

The next two theorems give the basic recursion formulae for the while and repeat forms of iteration.

3.3(6) Theorem (While-loop Recursion). $P?A = P \rightarrow A \cdot (P?A)/I$

Proof.

$P?A = (P \rightarrow A/Z)^* \cdot (P \rightarrow Z/I)$ by Def. 1.5(4)

$= (I \cup (P \rightarrow A/Z) \cdot (P \rightarrow A/Z)^*) \cdot (P \rightarrow Z/I)$ by 3.1(4)

$= I \cdot (P \rightarrow Z/I) \cup (P \rightarrow A/Z) \cdot (P \rightarrow A/Z)^* \cdot (P \rightarrow Z/I)$ by 3.1(6)

$= (P \rightarrow Z/I) \cup (P \rightarrow A/Z) \cdot (P?A)$

$= P \rightarrow Z/I \cup P \rightarrow A \cdot (P?A)/Z$ by 3.2(5)

$= P \rightarrow A \cdot (P?A)/I$ by 3.2(9)(iii). □

3.3(7) Theorem (Repeat-loop Recursion). $A!P = A \cdot (P \rightarrow I/(A!P))$

Proof.

$A!P = A \cdot (\underline{\text{not}}\ P\ ?A)$ by Def. 2.2(3)

$= A \cdot (\underline{\text{not}}\ P \rightarrow A \cdot (\underline{\text{not}}\ P\ ?A)/I)$ by 3.3(6)

$= A \cdot (\underline{\text{not}}\ P \rightarrow (A!P)/I)$

$= A \cdot (P \rightarrow I/(A!P))$ by 3.2(2). □

3. Properties of Relators

Corollary 1.5(8) gave P?A as a special case of the guarded command form of iteration. The theorem which follows gives conditions under which the latter may be reduced to the former.

3.3(8) Theorem. If $P_1,\dots,P_n$ are all total predicates, then

$$\underline{\text{do}}\ P_1 \rightarrow A_1 \,[]\, \dots \,[]\, P_n \rightarrow A_n\ \underline{\text{od}} = Q?B$$

where

$Q = P_1\ \underline{\text{or}}\ \dots\ \underline{\text{or}}\ P_n$, and

$B = \underline{\text{if}}\ P_1 \rightarrow A_1 \,[]\, \dots \,[]\, P_n \rightarrow A_n\ \underline{\text{fi}}$.

Proof.

$\underline{\text{do}}\ P_1 \rightarrow A_1 \,[]\, \dots \,[]\, P_n \rightarrow A_n\ \underline{\text{od}}$

$= (P_1 \rightarrow A_1/Z \cup \dots \cup P_n \rightarrow A_n/Z)^* \cdot (P_1 \rightarrow Z/I \cap \dots \cap P_n \rightarrow Z/I)$ by 1.5(7).

Also,

$x(P_1 \rightarrow Z/I \cap \dots \cap P_n \rightarrow Z/I)y$

$\iff x(P_1 \rightarrow Z/I)y \wedge \dots \wedge x(P_n \rightarrow Z/I)y$ by 1.3(1)

$\iff xP_1f \wedge \dots \wedge xP_nf \wedge y=x$

$\iff x(Q \rightarrow Z/I)y$,

since xQf holds if and only if xP_jf is true for each of the j. Thus, by 3.2(7)

$$\underline{\text{do}}\ P_1 \rightarrow A_1 \,[]\, \dots \,[]\, P_n \rightarrow A_n\ \underline{\text{od}} = B^* \cdot (Q \rightarrow Z/I). \qquad (*)$$

But

$x(Q \rightarrow B/Z)y$

$\iff xQt \wedge xBy$

$\iff xBy$

since Q:x=t must be true for B to be applicable to x. Thus we can write $(Q \rightarrow B/Z)$ in place of B in equation (*), completing the proof. □

The final two theorems of this section belong to a family of theorems that are important in optimization. They concern the conditions under which a relator may be moved outside a loop. A simple example from programming would be the Pascal [13] statement

<u>repeat</u> n:=0; read(ch) <u>until</u> ch = '*'

which sets n to zero and skips characters on the input file to the next asterisk. Obviously, the "n:=0" can be taken out of the loop and put either before or after it without making any difference except to the speed of execution. At a higher level of program sophistication, one may say that an important difference between a compiler and an interpreter for a given language is that the compiler moves operations out of the execution loop and performs them before the loop is entered. Before proving the two loop optimization theorems, we must make some preparations.

3.3(9) Lemma. If P is deterministic

$$P\to(P\to A/B)/C = P\to A/C.$$

Proof.

$x(P\to(P\to A/B)/C)y$

$\iff xPt \wedge x(P\to A/B)y \vee xPf \wedge xCy$

$\iff xPt \wedge (xPt \wedge xAy \vee xPf \wedge xBy) \vee xPf \wedge xCy$

$\iff xPt \wedge xAy \vee xPf \wedge xCy$ since xPt and xPf cannot both hold

$\iff x(P\to A/C)y$ □

3.3(10) Definition. The relators P, A and B satisfy the loop optimization conditions if and only if

(i) P and A are deterministic,

(ii) $A\cdot A = A$ (that is, A is idempotent),

(iii) $A\cdot P = P$,

(iv) $A\cdot B\cdot A = A\cdot B$.

Notice that if conditions (i), (ii) and (iii) are satisfied and $A\cdot B = B\cdot A$, then condition (iv) is satisfied, since $A\cdot B\cdot A = A\cdot A\cdot B = A\cdot B$ by condition (ii). On the other hand, condition (iv) does not imply that A and B commute, as can be seen by putting $A=T$ and $B=I\to I/Z$.

3.3(11) Lemma. If P, A and B satisfy the loop optimization conditions, then

$$(P\to A\cdot B/Z)^+ = A\cdot(P\to B/Z)^+$$

where we define $C^+ = C\cdot C^*$, so that $xC^+y \iff (\exists n)(xC^{n+1}y)$ for non-negative n.

Proof. First prove by induction on n that

$$(P\rightarrow A\cdot B/Z)^n = A\cdot(P\rightarrow B/Z)^n$$

for all n>0.

For n=1 we have

$P\rightarrow A\cdot B/Z$

$= A\cdot P\rightarrow A\cdot B/A\cdot Z$ by 3.3(10)(iii) and 3.1(1)

$= A\cdot(P\rightarrow B/Z)$ by 3.2(6).

Assume the result is true for n=j. Then

$(P\rightarrow A\cdot B/Z)^{j+1}$

$= (P\rightarrow A\cdot B/Z)\cdot(P\rightarrow A\cdot B/Z)^j$

$= (P\rightarrow A\cdot B/Z)\cdot A\cdot(P\rightarrow B/Z)^j$ by ind. hyp.

$= (P\rightarrow A\cdot B\cdot A/Z)\cdot(P\rightarrow B/Z)^j$ by 3.2(5)

$= (A\cdot P\rightarrow A\cdot B/A\cdot Z)\cdot(P\rightarrow B/Z)^j$ by 3.3(10)(iii) and (iv)

$= A\cdot(P\rightarrow B/Z)\cdot(P\rightarrow B/Z)^j$

$= A\cdot(P\rightarrow B/Z)^{j+1}$.

Now

$x(P\rightarrow A\cdot B/Z)^+y$

$\iff (\exists n)(x(P\rightarrow A\cdot B/Z)^{n+1}y)$

$\iff (\exists n)(xA\cdot(P\rightarrow B/Z)^{n+1}y)$

$\iff (\exists n)(\exists z)(xAz \wedge z(P\rightarrow B/Z)^{n+1}y)$

$\iff (\exists z)(xAz \wedge (\exists n)(z(P\rightarrow B/Z)^{n+1}y))$ by A2, A6

$\iff (\exists z)(xAz \wedge z(P\rightarrow B/Z)^+y)$

$\iff xA\cdot(P\rightarrow B/Z)^+y$

as required. □

3.3(12) Lemma. If P is deterministic

$$P?A = P\rightarrow(P\rightarrow A/Z)^+\cdot(P\rightarrow Z/I)/I.$$

Proof.

$P?A = P\rightarrow A\cdot(P?A)/I$ by 3.3(6)

$= P\rightarrow(P\rightarrow A\cdot(P?A)/Z)/I$ by 3.3(9)

$= P\rightarrow(P\rightarrow A/Z)\cdot(P?A)/I$ by 3.2(5)

$= P\rightarrow(P\rightarrow A/Z)\cdot(P\rightarrow A/Z)^*\cdot(P\rightarrow Z/I)/I$ by 1.5(4)

$= P\rightarrow(P\rightarrow A/Z)^+\cdot(P\rightarrow Z/I)/I$ □

3.3(13) Theorem (While-loop Optimization). If P, A and B satisfy the loop optimization conditions,

$$P?(A\cdot B) = P\rightarrow A\cdot(P?B)/I.$$

Proof.

$P\rightarrow A\cdot(P?B)/I$

$= P\rightarrow A\cdot(P\rightarrow(P\rightarrow B/Z)^{+}\cdot(P\rightarrow Z/I)/I)/I$ by 3.3(12)

$= P\rightarrow(P\rightarrow A\cdot(P\rightarrow B/Z)^{+}\cdot(P\rightarrow Z/I)/A)/I$

by 3.3(10)(iii) and 3.2(6)

$= P\rightarrow(P\rightarrow(P\rightarrow A\cdot B/Z)^{+}\cdot(P\rightarrow Z/I)/A)/I$ by 3.3(11)

$= P\rightarrow(P\rightarrow A\cdot B/Z)^{+}\cdot(P\rightarrow Z/I)/I$ by 3.3(9)

$= P?(A\cdot B)$ by 3.3(12). □

3.3(14) Theorem (Repeat-loop Optimization). If P, A and B satisfy the loop optimization conditions, and B is deterministic,

$$(A\cdot B)!P = A\cdot(B!P).$$

Proof. Let Q = not P. We shall prove, first of all, that if P, A and B satisfy the loop optimization conditions, Q, A and B do also. We have $Q = P\rightarrow F/T$, so that Q is deterministic; we also need to show that $A\cdot Q = Q$.

$A\cdot Q = A\cdot(P\rightarrow F/T)$

$= A\cdot P\rightarrow A\cdot F/A\cdot T$

$= P\rightarrow A\cdot F/A\cdot T$

This will be equal to $P\rightarrow F/T$, as required, provided there is no value of x for which $P:x \in \{t,f\}$ while A:x is undefined. But since $P:x = A\cdot P:x$, it is not possible for P:x to be defined when A:x is not.

$(A\cdot B)!P$

$= A\cdot B\cdot(Q?(A\cdot B))$ by 2.2(3)

$= A\cdot B\cdot(Q\rightarrow A\cdot(Q?B)/I)$ by 3.3(13)

$= A\cdot B\cdot(Q\rightarrow A\cdot(Q\rightarrow B\cdot(Q?B)/I)/I)$ by 3.3(6)

$= A\cdot B\cdot(Q\rightarrow(A\cdot Q\rightarrow A\cdot B\cdot(Q?B)/A)/I)$ by 3.2(6)

$= A\cdot B\cdot(Q\rightarrow(Q\rightarrow A\cdot B\cdot(Q?B)/A)/I)$ by hyp.

$= A\cdot B\cdot(Q\rightarrow A\cdot B\cdot(Q?B)/I)$ by 3.3(9)

$= A\cdot B\cdot Q\rightarrow A\cdot B\cdot A\cdot B\cdot(Q?B)/A\cdot B$ by 3.2(6)

$= A \cdot B \cdot Q \rightarrow A \cdot B \cdot B \cdot (Q?B)/A \cdot B$ by hyp.
$= A \cdot B \cdot (Q \rightarrow B \cdot (Q?B)/I)$ by 3.2(6)
$= A \cdot B \cdot (Q?B)$ by 3.3(6)
$= A \cdot (B!P)$ by 2.2(3).□

It is worth looking at the conditions of 3.3(10) more closely. The idempotence condition, A•A=A, means that after one execution of A, subsequent executions have no further effect. (The situation would be entirely different in the repeat statement of the example before Theorem 3.3(9) if we had "n:=n+1" instead of "n:=0".) The fourth condition is related to idempotence: after execution of A and then B, subsequent executions of A have no further effect. The other condition, A•P=P, means that P, which must be a predicate if Theorems 3.3(13) and 3.3(14) are not to be vacuous, is independent of A.

3.4 Construction Operations

In this section we shall look at some of the properties of the data handling components of RW^+. This part of the calculus is specific to the base set W, so that the results obtained will be much less general than those of the previous sections. For a discussion of n-tuples of arbitrary length, the reader is referred to [1].

3.4(1) Theorem.

(i) $\langle A,B \rangle \cdot X \subseteq A$

(ii) $\langle A,B \rangle \cdot Y \subseteq B$

Proof (of part (i) only).

The result of applying <A,B> to x is a pair <u,v> such that xAu and xBv, provided both A and B are applicable to x. Application of X to this yields u, that is, the same result as is obtained by applying A. However, since both A and B must be applicable for this result to be obtained, <A,B>•X may not be applicable in some cases where A is. □

3. Properties of Relators

The following two theorems indicate the extent to which composition and the conditional distribute over the construction operation.

3.4(2) <u>Theorem</u>. $A\cdot\langle B,C\rangle \subseteq \langle A\cdot B,A\cdot C\rangle$, with equality holding when A is deterministic.

<u>Proof</u>.

$x(A\cdot\langle B,C\rangle)y$

$$\iff (\exists z)(xAz \wedge z\langle B,C\rangle y)$$

$$\iff (\exists z)(xAz \wedge (\exists u)(\exists v)(zBu \wedge zCv \wedge y=\langle u,v\rangle)$$

$$\iff (\exists u)(\exists v)(\exists z)(xAz \wedge zBu \wedge xAz \wedge zCv \wedge y=\langle u,v\rangle) \qquad \text{by A2, A6}$$

$$\Longrightarrow (\exists u)(\exists v)((\exists z)(xAz \wedge zBu) \wedge (\exists z)(xAz \wedge zCv) \wedge y=\langle u,v\rangle) \qquad \text{by A5}$$

$$\iff (\exists u)(\exists v)(x(A\cdot B)u \wedge x(A\cdot C)v \wedge y=\langle u,v\rangle)$$

$$\iff x\langle A\cdot B,A\cdot C\rangle y$$

If A is non-deterministic there may be several z satisfying xAz, but there may be no one of these which satisfies both zBu and zCv; thus the fifth line is only an implication. If A is deterministic, on the other hand, there is at most one z satisfying xAz and this problem does not arise: line 5 is an equivalence, and equality holds in the statement of the theorem.

To see that equality does not always hold we may use a counter-example suggested by Bruce Southcott: put $A=(T\cup F)$, $B=C=I$. Then $A\cdot\langle B,C\rangle$ may yield either $\langle t,t\rangle$ or $\langle f,f\rangle$ when applied to an arbitrary element of W, whereas $\langle A\cdot B,A\cdot C\rangle$ may yield any of the four combinations of t and f. □

3.4(3) <u>Theorem</u>.

(i) $\langle P\to A/B,\ C\rangle = P\to\langle A,C\rangle/\langle B,C\rangle$

(ii) $\langle A,\ P\to B/C\rangle = P\to\langle A,B\rangle/\langle A,C\rangle$

3.4(4) <u>Theorem</u>. $\langle A,B\rangle\cdot\langle X\cdot C,Y\cdot D\rangle = \langle A\cdot C,B\cdot D\rangle$

<u>Proof</u>.

Since applications of $\langle A,B\rangle$ and $\langle X\cdot C,Y\cdot D\rangle$ necessarily yield pairs, we may modify 1.2(1) to give

$$z(\langle A\cdot B\rangle\cdot\langle X\cdot C, Y\cdot D\rangle)\langle x,y\rangle$$
$$\iff (\exists u)(\exists v)(z\langle A,B\rangle\langle u,v\rangle \wedge \langle u,v\rangle\langle X\cdot C,Y\cdot D\rangle\langle x,y\rangle)$$
$$\iff (\exists u)(\exists v)(zAu\wedge zBv \wedge uCx\wedge vDy)$$
$$\iff (\exists u)(zAu\wedge uCx) \wedge (\exists v)(zBv\wedge vDy) \qquad \text{by A2}$$
$$\iff zA\cdot Cx \wedge zB\cdot Dy$$
$$\iff z\langle A\cdot C,B\cdot D\rangle\langle x,y\rangle \qquad \square$$

A number of special cases are obtainable from this theorem by making substitutions for A, B, C and D. For example

$$\langle X\cdot A,\ Y\rangle\cdot\langle X,\ Y\cdot B\rangle = \langle X\cdot A,\ Y\cdot B\rangle.$$

The theorem is used in proving an important result concerning iteration, 4.2(13).

3.5 Recursion

In this section we shall examine the questions of the existence and uniqueness of solutions to sets of equations like those of Section 1.7. I shall outline the existence proof, which makes use of the theory of functions on complete lattices. An account of this theory may be found, for example, in [29] or [23].

3.5(1) Notation. Given a base set S and some positive integer n, we shall

(i) denote by $\underline{y}$ a vector $[y_1,\ldots,y_n]$ in S^n;

(ii) denote by $\underline{A}$ a vector of relators $[A_1,\ldots,A_n]$ in $\mathrm{Rel}(S)^n$, with $\underline{Z} = [Z,\ldots,Z]$;

(iii) write $x\underline{A}\underline{y}$ to indicate that $xA_j y_j$ holds for all j; and

(iv) denote by $\underline{E}$ the function $\underline{E}:\mathrm{Rel}(S)^n\to\mathrm{Rel}(S)^n$ which maps $\underline{A}$ into $\underline{B}$ as shown:

$$B_1 = E_1(A_1,\ldots,A_n),$$
$$B_2 = E_2(A_1,\ldots,A_n),$$
$$\cdot\ \cdot\ \cdot\ \cdot\ \cdot\ \cdot\ ,$$
$$B_n = E_n(A_1,\ldots,A_n),$$

where the E_j are relator-valued functions, $E_j:\mathrm{Rel}(S)^n\to\mathrm{Rel}(S)$.

3. Properties of Relators

We may now restate our problem. Given n relator expressions in the relator variables $A_1,\ldots,A_n$ which define the functions $E_1,\ldots,E_n$ we ask whether $\underline{A}=\underline{E}(\underline{A})$ has a solution, and if in fact there are several solutions, whether one of them is in some sense unique. The answer is provided by Theorem 6.64 of [29], which tells us that if $Rel(S)^n$ is a complete lattice, and if $\underline{E}$ is a continuous function on that lattice, then $\underline{E}$ has a minimal fixed point (which is specified in the theorem). On the basis of this result we may assert the following theorem.

3.5(2) Theorem. If all the functions comprising $\underline{E}$ are defined by expressions in RW^+ the equation $\underline{A}=\underline{E}(\underline{A})$ has a minimal solution which satisfies

$$(\forall x)(\forall \underline{y})(x\underline{A}\,\underline{y} \iff (\exists j)(x\underline{E}^j(\underline{Z})\underline{y})).$$

Proof.

An outline of the six steps in the proof is first given (in the paragraphs numbered 1 to 6 which follow) and then step 2, which is specifically concerned with RW^+ is treated in more detail.

1. Rel(W) is a complete lattice under the ordering $\subseteq$.
2. All the relational operations of RW^+ are functions on Rel(W); for example, P?A corresponds to a function $Rel(W)^2 \to Rel(W)$. Show that each of these operations is continuous in each of its variables taken separately; it will follow by Theorem 6.53 of [29] that they are continuous on the variables taken together.
3. The expressions comprising each E_j are formed by composition of relational operations. By Theorem 6.54 of [29] these expressions define continuous functions on $A_1,\ldots,A_n$.
4. Construct the product lattice $Rel(W)^n$ using the partial ordering of 6.31 in [29]. (According to this ordering, $\underline{A}$ is stronger than $\underline{B}$ if each element of $\underline{A}$ is stronger than the corresponding element of $\underline{B}$.)
5. Continuity of $\underline{E}$ follows by Theorem 3.16 of [23].
6. The existence and value of the fixed point are given by 6.63 and 6.64 of [29].

3. Properties of Relators

In most cases, the relational operations are not only continuous in their variables, but also completely additive - a property that is stronger than continuity, but easier to prove. I will illustrate the method of proof by showing that P→A/B is completely additive in the variable P, that is to say, that if R is an arbitrary, non-empty set of relators,

$$\bigcup_{P \in R} (P \to A/B) = (\bigcup_{P \in R} P) \to A/B.$$

We have

$x(\cup (P \to A/B))y$

$\iff (\exists P)(P \in R \wedge x(P \to A/B)y)$

$\iff (\exists P)(P \in R \wedge (xPt \wedge xAy \vee xPf \wedge xBy))$

$\iff (\exists P)((P \in R \wedge xPt \wedge xAy) \vee (P \in R \wedge xPf \wedge xBy))$

$\iff (\exists P)(P \in R \wedge xPt) \wedge xAy \vee (\exists P)(P \in R \wedge xPf) \wedge xBy$

$\iff x(\cup P)t \wedge xAy \vee x(\cup P)f \wedge xBy$

$\iff (\cup P) \to A/B,$

so that complete additivity holds in this case.

The only operation that does not yield to this kind of treatment is the star operation of 1.3(2). However, if we rewrite this as

$$A^* = \bigcup_{n=0}^{\infty} A^n$$

and notice that the A^n are continuous functions of A, we conclude that A* is also a continuous function of A, since the set of continuous functions forms a complete lattice, so that the least upper bound of a subset of this set is a continuous function. □

To see the practical significance of this theorem I shall again use the example of Q = P→B·Q/I which defines Q to be P?B. Since there is only one recursive equation, our notation may be simplified to

$$E(A) = P \to B \cdot A/I.$$

3. Properties of Relators

The sequence of relators $\langle E^j(Z)\rangle$ is

$$E^0(Z) = Z$$
$$E^1(Z) = P \rightarrow B \cdot Z/I$$
$$E^2(Z) = P \rightarrow B \cdot (P \rightarrow B \cdot Z/I)/I$$
$$E^3(Z) = P \rightarrow B \cdot (P \rightarrow B \cdot (P \rightarrow B \cdot Z/I)/I)/I$$
$$\cdot \quad \cdot \quad \cdot \quad \cdot \quad \cdot \quad \cdot \quad \cdot \quad \cdot \quad \cdot \quad \cdot \quad \cdot$$

where $E^{j+1}(Z)$ is obtained by substituting $E^j(Z)$ for A in $P \rightarrow B \cdot A/I$.

According to 3.5(2), xQy holds if and only if there is some non-negative j such that $xE^j(Z)y$. Suppose, for a particular x, we have

$$xPt,\ x(B \cdot P)t,\ x(B^2 \cdot P)f,\ \ldots$$

so that we would expect application of P?B to have the effect of applying B twice. Then we find that application of $E^0(Z)$, $E^1(Z)$, and $E^2(Z)$ to x are all undefined, but application of $E^3(Z)$ (and all subsequent terms) has the same effect as applying B^2. And, in general, if application of P?B to x involves i iterations, $E^{i+1}(Z)$ is the first relator in the sequence to be applicable.

Needless to say, we do not solve the recursion $\underline{A} = \underline{E}(\underline{A})$ in practice by applying successive expansions of $\underline{E}^n$ to an operand. Instead, we make use of an iterative process in which textual nesting is replaced by dynamic nesting using a stack. But if we wish to have confidence in the correctness of the result, we need to be able to show that the iteration is equivalent to the process I have outlined here.

The theorem asserts that the solution given is the minimal fixed point. Consider the single equation case, and suppose that $A=E(A)$ and $A'=E(A')$ both hold, and that A is the minimal fixed point. This means simply, in our lattice, that $A \subseteq A'$, which in turn means that if for any input-output pair $\langle x,y\rangle$ xAy holds, then xA′y holds also. On the other hand, there will be pairs $\langle x',y'\rangle$ for which x′A′y′ holds, but not x′Ay′; they will satisfy A′ but not A, nor, for that matter, other non-minimal fixed point relators. Such input-output pairs are therefore not fully determined by E, and must be regarded as spurious. The minimal fixed point contains all those, and only those, input-output pairs which are fully determined by E.

Chapter 4. THE EXTENSION OF A CALCULUS

A major development in computing over the last two decades has been the production of languages which are extensible in the sense that they enable the programmer to define new data types along with the operators needed to manipulate them.

In this chapter and Chapter 5 we shall study the corresponding extension process for relational calculi. The techniques used will be basically those which are, by now, well known to language designers, but the application area will be rather different. Instead of working with a programming language, which is a representation of a relational calculus, we shall be working directly with the calculus itself, and what is more, we shall not be encumbered by many of the constraints which surround the designer of a practical language.

4.1 Proper and Virtual Extensions

We may distinguish between a proper extension and a virtual extension of a relational calculus.

In a proper extension new elements are added to the base set, and new primitive relators and (possibly) relational operations are included in the calculus. For example, the set of non-negative integers and the successor operation are defined by Peano's Postulates. Thus we might extend RW by allowing an atom to be either t, f or a non-negative integer, so that an arbitrary element of the base set would be a binary tree having these atomic elements as terminal nodes. As additional primitive relators we would need the successor function and a zero test. (Notice particularly that we are not speaking of adding any representation of the non-negative integers here, but of the integers themselves - the abstract set defined by Peano's Postulates. It is essential to maintain this distinction between an object and its representation when studying data types.)

In a virtual extension, the elements of the new data type are represented by elements of the existing base set without actually adding any new elements to it. The operations of the new data type are implemented by using the previously defined relators of the calculus to manipulate the representations. And in some cases this process may go to the extent of reproducing one relational calculus within another; this happens when the complete base set of the first is represented within the second, and all its primitive relators and relational operations are implemented. When this is the case, anything that can be done in the first calculus can equally well be done in the second. Before going on to look at an example of all this in Section 4.2 we must clarify the meanings of the terms we have been using.

4.1(1) Definition. Let R and S be two sets and let Abst:R→S be a function from R into S. Then we say that Abst defines a representation of S in R; if Abst(r)=s we say that r represents s, and conversely that s is an abstraction of r. If Abst is a function onto S, Abst defines a total representation.

As an example, let us look at the representation of the non-negative integers by the binary numerals. The syntax of the numerals is given by

Numeral n ::= 0 | 1 | n0 | n1

We will denote the number zero in Peano's Postulates by "zero" (to avoid confusion with the numeral "0"), the successor function by "successor" and the function which doubles its argument by "twice". Then, using the notation of denotational semantics (see Stoy [29], Chapter 3) we may define the function Abst recursively by

(1) Abst⟦0⟧ = zero,

(2) Abst⟦1⟧ = successor(zero),

(3) Abst⟦n0⟧ = twice(Abst⟦n⟧),

(4) Abst⟦n1⟧ = successor(twice(Abst⟦n⟧)).

In these equations we have followed the practice of denotational semantics by enclosing elements of the representation set in the hollow brackets ⟦ ⟧.

To see how the equations work, consider the example of the binary numeral "10". By equation (3) we have Abst⟦10⟧ = twice(Abst⟦1⟧), and by (1), Abst⟦1⟧ = successor(zero) so that,

Abst⟦10⟧ = twice(successor(zero)).

It is clear that this method may be used to map any binary numeral (that is, any string of 0's and 1's) into an expression in "zero", "successor" and "twice", which in turn evaluates to a non-negative integer, so that, effectively, we have completely defined the function Abst for this particular representation.

Since Abst is a function it denotes a many-one mapping. This corresponds to the representations that occur in practice: "10" represents a unique non-negative integer, but "010", "0010" and so on represent the same integer.

We have only required Abst to be a function into S, not onto S, so it is possible that some elements of S are not represented. This occurs in practice when, for example, only a finite subset of the integers can be represented in the arithmetic of a particular computer.

My intention in introducing the term "abstraction" as the inverse of "representation" was to point out that there are, in fact, two complementary ways of looking at the process. If our primary interest is in the abstract set of objects, the non-negative integers, then Abst defines one of many possible representations. But if our interest is centred on strings of bits then Abst provides one of many possible ways of mapping the individual strings into abstract objects; in practice, many alternative abstractions are provided for the bit strings held in a computer memory - integers, reals, character strings and so on. I will return to this subject in Section 5.4, where, in particular, the reason for choosing the term "abstraction" should become clearer.

It is a little more difficult to define implementation than representation. To be fully general, we should consider the implementation of a relator or function in which both the range and domain are Cartesian products involving othe· sets in addition to S. However, this has the effect of adding a great deal of notational complexity to what is in essence a simple idea, so I shall only describe the implementation of a dyadic relator, leaving it to the reader to adapt the definition to other cases. (One such adaptation occurs in 6.1(2).)

4.1(2) Definition. Let R, S and Abst be defined as in 4.1(1) and let $A \subseteq R^2$ and $B \subseteq S^2$ be relators on R and S respectively. Then A is an implementation of B if and only if, for all x and y in the domain of Abst,

$$xAy \Longrightarrow \text{Abst}(x)\ B\ \text{Abst}(y).$$

This definition guarantees that A is a correct implementation of B as far as it goes: if A is applicable to some element x, then the result obtained is a representation of a result obtainable by applying B to the abstraction of x. On the other hand, it does not guarantee that there is a computation of A corresponding to every computation that can be performed by B. A may only be a partial implementation of B, and in fact, according to this definition, the null relator Z on R is a (vacuous) implementation of every relator on S. Nevertheless, the definition corresponds reasonably well to computing practice: we do not refuse to say that the integer add instruction of a computer implements the sum function because it is only applicable to numbers within the integer range of the machine. However, it is clearly desirable to be able to distinguish between the (partial) implementation we have been discussing and a total implementation.

4.1(3) <u>Definition</u>. The implementation A of B is <u>total</u> if and only if

$$(\forall u \in S)(\forall v \in S)(uBv \Longrightarrow (\exists x \in R)(\exists y \in R)(u=Abst(x) \wedge v=Abst(y) \wedge xAy)).$$

The effect of this is that every input-output pair of B is mirrored by at least one input-output pair of A. (It may be noted in passing that representation and implementation as defined here are closely related to homomorphism in algebra.)

We return, finally, to the idea of a reproduction of a calculus which was introduced earlier. Suppose we have two calculi with base sets R and S respectively. Then to reproduce the calculus on S within the calculus on R we must satisfy three conditions:

(i) There is a function Abst defining a total representation of S within R.

(ii) All the primitive relators of the calculus on S have total implementations in R.

(iii) There must be some construction in the calculus on R corresponding to each relational operation of the other calculus, so that, for each relator expression on S, there is a relator expression on R which implements it.

If these conditions are satisfied it is clear that any relator computable in the calculus on S is also computable in the calculus on R. This principle will be used in Theorems 8.1(1) and 8.1(2) to determine the functions computable in RW.

4.2 An Example: The Non-Negative Integers in RW

In this section we shall see how a virtual extension of RW may be defined to provide a representation of the non-negative integers and implementations of a number of important integer functions. This will serve as an example of the ideas discussed in the last section and, at the same time, provide valuable facilities for RW.

When attacking any problem it is worth while trying to factorize it into component problems; as far as possible, one tries to unravel the distinct strands of the problem and deal with them one at a time. In the present case we may distinguish two strands: producing a correct treatment of the integers, and producing an efficient one. The two are not entirely independent; as one modifies an implementation to make it more efficient it usually becomes harder to establish correctness. Nevertheless, it is worth while studying a simple system, leaving aside the question of efficiency, since the handling of correctness proofs in this case can serve as a model when deriving proofs in more complex cases. There is another point, too. When dealing with questions of computability we are concerned to know that certain functions can be implemented in a calculus without being at all interested in how they are implemented. The treatment of integers that follows is entirely adequate for this purpose.

The representation of the non-negative integers used here will be simpler than the binary representation which was used as an example in Section 4.1, but it will again be defined recursively.

4.2(1) Definition. The numerals used to represent the non-negative integers in RW are defined by

(i) <f,f> represents zero;

(ii) if the element x of W represents the integer j, then <t,x> represents the successor of j; and

(iii) only those elements of W are numerals which are required to be by (i) and (ii).

4.2(2) <u>Definition</u>. The relator Succ in RW is given by

Succ = <T,I>.

I shall denote the RW numeral corresponding to the non-negative integer j by $\overline{j}$. Thus $\overline{0}$=<f,f>, $\overline{1}$=<t,<f,f>> and so on. The theorem which follows validates our extension of RW since Peano's Postulates define the non-negative integers and the successor function.

4.2(3) <u>Theorem</u>. The numerals defined in 4.2(1) satisfy Peano's Postulates provided the relator Succ of 4.2(2) is taken as the successor function.

<u>Proof</u>.

I shall use the version of the Postulates given in Mendelson [18], substituting "numeral" for "natural number" and Succ(x) for x′.

(P1) $\overline{0}$ is a numeral. - Given by 4.2(1)(i).

(P2) If $\overline{x}$ is a numeral, then Succ:$\overline{x}$ is a numeral. - Succ:$\overline{x}$ = <t,$\overline{x}$>, which is the representation of the successor of x, by 4.2(1)(ii).

(P3) $\overline{0} \neq$ Succ:$\overline{x}$ for any numeral $\overline{x}$. - <f,f>=<t,$\overline{x}$> is impossible by 1.6(1)(iv).

(P4) If Succ:$\overline{x}$ = Succ:$\overline{y}$ then $\overline{x}$ = $\overline{y}$. - That is, if <t,$\overline{x}$> = <t,$\overline{y}$> then $\overline{x}$ = $\overline{y}$; this again follows from 1.6(1)(iv).

(P5) The Principle of Induction: If a property Q holds for $\overline{0}$ and, whenever it holds for $\overline{x}$ it also holds for Succ($\overline{x}$), then it holds for all numerals. - According to 4.2(1), every numeral $\overline{x}$ has the form

<t,<t,...<t,<f,f>>...>>

where x is the number of t's in the numeral; this follows immediately from (i) and (ii) by induction on the integer represented, together with the fact that by (iii) only elements of this form are numerals. Thus 4.2(1) defines an isomorphism between the numerals and the non-negative integer, with Succ corresponding to the successor function, so that we can replace induction on the numerals by an induction on the non-negative integers. □

4.2(4) <u>Corollary</u>. Definition 4.2(1) gives a total representation of the non-negative integers and 4.2(2) a total implementation of the successor function.

Having established a valid basis for our extension, we may now implement some of the more important numerical functions, starting with the constant relators for the numerals.

4.2(5) <u>Definition</u>. The constant relators which yield the numerals are defined by

(i) $\overline{\overline{0}} = \langle F,F\rangle$,

(ii) $\overline{\overline{n+1}} = \langle T,\overline{\overline{n}}\rangle$.

For any non-negative integer n and any element x of W, $\overline{\overline{n}}{:}x = \overline{n}$.

4.2(6) <u>Definition</u>.

(i) Nonzero = X

(ii) Pred = Nonzero→Y/I

4.2(7) <u>Corollary</u>.

(i) $\text{Nonzero}{:}\overline{x} = f$ if $x=0$,
$= t$ otherwise.

(ii) $\text{Pred}{:}\overline{x} = \overline{x \dot{-} 1}$,

where $i \dot{-} j$ is the <u>proper difference</u> of i and j, defined by

$i \dot{-} j = i-j$ if $i>j$,
$= 0$ otherwise.

The alias "Nonzero" is provided for X in order to make relator expressions which operate on the numerals more intelligible. Proofs for 4.2(7) follow directly from 4.2(1).

The definitions of the other numeric functions may be simplified considerably by introducing a relational operation corresponding to the <u>for</u> statement of the programming languages.

4. Extension of a Calculus

We already have the equivalent of <u>for</u> i := 1 <u>to</u> n <u>do</u> S available to us as A^n in cases where n is a constant (and the statement S does not involve the variable i). If the value of n is not constant it can only be introduced as part of the operand. This is provided for in the definition which follows - but it still does not give access to the controlled variable i from within A.

4.2(8) <u>Definition</u>. $A\# = (Y{\cdot}Nonzero\ ?\ \langle X{\cdot}A,\ Y{\cdot}Pred\rangle){\cdot}X$

The effect of applying A# to an operand $\langle x,\overline{n}\rangle$ is, as we shall see shortly, to compute $A^n{:}x$. For example,

$$\langle I,F\rangle\#{:}\langle t,\overline{3}\rangle = \langle\langle\langle t,f\rangle,f\rangle,f\rangle$$

since $\langle I,F\rangle$ has the effect of replacing x by $\langle x,f\rangle$.

The next theorem is the recursion theorem for this type of iteration corresponding to the theorems 3.3(6) and 3.3(7) for the <u>while</u> and <u>repeat</u> forms. This is an important result in its own right, but is also required for 4.2(10), where we shall show that $A\#{:}\langle x,\overline{n}\rangle = A^n{:}x$. In proving both these theorems we shall use the abbreviations,

$P = Y{\cdot}Nonzero$, and

$M = \langle X{\cdot}A,\ Y{\cdot}Pred\rangle$,

so that we have $A\# = (P?M){\cdot}X$, and

$P{:}\langle x,\overline{n}\rangle = t$ if $n\neq 0$, and

$= f$ if $n=0$; and

$M{:}\langle x,\overline{n+1}\rangle = \langle A{:}x,\overline{n}\rangle$.

4.2(9) <u>Theorem</u>. $A\# = Y{\cdot}Nonzero \rightarrow \langle X{\cdot}A,\ Y{\cdot}Pred\rangle{\cdot}A\#/X$

<u>Proof</u>.

$A\# = (P?M){\cdot}X$

$= (P\rightarrow M{\cdot}(P?M)/I){\cdot}X$ by 3.3(6)

$= P\rightarrow M{\cdot}(P?M){\cdot}X/I{\cdot}X$ by 3.2(5)

$= P\rightarrow M{\cdot}A\#/X$ □

4.2(10) <u>Theorem</u>. $A\#{:}\langle x,\overline{n}\rangle = A^n{:}x$.

<u>Proof</u> by induction on n.

If n=0 then

$A\#:\langle x,\overline{0}\rangle$

$= X:\langle x,\overline{0}\rangle$ by 4.2(9) since $P:\langle x,\overline{0}\rangle = f$

$= x$

$= A^0:x.$

Suppose the statement is true for n=j. Then

$A\#:\langle x,\overline{j+1}\rangle$

$= M\cdot A\#:\langle x,\overline{j+1}\rangle$ by 4.2(9) since $P:\langle x,\overline{j+1}\rangle = t$

$= A\#:\langle A:x,\overline{j}\rangle$ applying M

$= A^j:(A:x)$ by the induction hypothesis

$= A\cdot A^j:x$

$= A^{j+1}:x$ □

The statement and proof of this theorem assume that A, and therefore A#, are deterministic relators - we could not write $A^n:x$, for example, if A were non-deterministic. This assumption is reasonable, since we are considering an extension of the calculus RW, where all relators are deterministic. If one wishes to include the A# operation in RW^+ the proof of 4.2(10) involves precisely the same steps, but the "first principles" logical notation must be used throughout.

Before going on to give implementations of other numeric functions it would be well to explain how all this fits in with the syntax of 2.2(1). We have extended the syntax in two ways. Firstly, we have introduced the constant relators of the form $\overline{\overline{n}}$. These may be accomodated by adding the alternative int to p (primitive). Secondly, we have the new relational operation of the form A#. This may be catered for by adding the alternative p# to the line for pwr (power). Apart from this, we have defined Succ, and will be defining other relators; all these can be placed at the beginning of the list of definitions in the where clause of an expression - they do not require any further syntactic extensions.

In Definition 4.2(11), each relator, as it is defined, is followed by a comment enclosed in braces indicating the effect of applying the relator.

4.2(11) Definition.

(i) Sum = Succ# $\{\mathrm{Sum}{:}\langle\overline{m},\overline{n}\rangle = \overline{m+n}\}$

(ii) Prdiff = Pred# $\{\mathrm{Prdiff}{:}\langle\overline{m},\overline{n}\rangle = \overline{m \dot{-} n}\}$

(iii) Prod = $\langle\langle X,\overline{\overline{0}}\rangle,Y\rangle\cdot\langle X,\mathrm{Sum}\rangle\#\cdot Y$ $\{\mathrm{Prod}{:}\langle\overline{m},\overline{n}\rangle = \overline{m\cdot n}\}$

(iv) Gt = Prdiff·Nonzero $\{\mathrm{Gt}{:}\langle\overline{m},\overline{n}\rangle = \underline{\text{if}}\ m>n\ \underline{\text{then}}\ t\ \underline{\text{else}}\ f\}$

Le = not Gt $\{\mathrm{Le}{:}\langle\overline{m},\overline{n}\rangle = \underline{\text{if}}\ m\leq n\ \underline{\text{then}}\ t\ \underline{\text{else}}\ f\}$

Lt = $\langle Y,X\rangle\cdot$Gt $\{\mathrm{Lt}{:}\langle\overline{m},\overline{n}\rangle = \underline{\text{if}}\ m<n\ \underline{\text{then}}\ t\ \underline{\text{else}}\ f\}$

Ge = not Lt $\{\mathrm{Ge}{:}\langle\overline{m},\overline{n}\rangle = \underline{\text{if}}\ m\geq n\ \underline{\text{then}}\ t\ \underline{\text{else}}\ f\}$

Eq = Le and Ge $\{\mathrm{Eq}{:}\langle\overline{m},\overline{n}\rangle = \underline{\text{if}}\ m=n\ \underline{\text{then}}\ t\ \underline{\text{else}}\ f\}$

Ne = Lt or Gt $\{\mathrm{Ne}{:}\langle\overline{m},\overline{n}\rangle = \underline{\text{if}}\ m\neq n\ \underline{\text{then}}\ t\ \underline{\text{else}}\ f\}$

(v) Quot = $\langle I,\overline{\overline{0}}\rangle\cdot(X\cdot\mathrm{Ge}?\langle X\cdot\langle\mathrm{Prdiff},Y\rangle,\ Y\cdot\mathrm{Succ}\rangle)\cdot Y$

$\{\mathrm{Quot}{:}\langle\overline{m},\overline{n}\rangle = \overline{m\ \mathrm{div}\ n}$ (integer division)$\}$

(vi) Rem = $(\mathrm{Ge}?\langle\mathrm{Prdiff},\ Y\rangle)\cdot X$

$\{\mathrm{Rem}{:}\langle\overline{m},\overline{n}\rangle$ gives the remainder on dividing m by n.$\}$

In number theory, the addition operator is defined in terms of the successor function by means of the recursion

$$x+0 = x$$
$$x+y' = (x+y)'$$

where x' denotes the successor of x. A similar definition is given for the multiplication operator. We shall verify that Sum, as defined above, satisfies this recursion, but will use a more intuitive approach for multiplication in order to bring out a parallel with the use of local variables in programming.

4.2(12) Theorem. The relator Sum of 4.2(11) satisfies

$$\mathrm{Sum}{:}\langle\overline{m},\overline{0}\rangle = \overline{m},$$
$$\mathrm{Sum}{:}\langle\overline{m},\mathrm{Succ}{:}\overline{n}\rangle = \mathrm{Succ}{:}\mathrm{Sum}{:}\langle\overline{m},\overline{n}\rangle.$$

Proof.

$\mathrm{Sum}{:}\langle\overline{m},\overline{0}\rangle = \mathrm{Succ}^0{:}\overline{m} = \overline{m}.$

$\mathrm{Sum}{:}\langle\overline{m},\mathrm{Succ}{:}\overline{n}\rangle$

$= \mathrm{Succ}^{n+1}{:}\overline{m}$ by 4.2(4) and 4.2(10)

$= \mathrm{Succ}{:}\mathrm{Succ}^{n}{:}\overline{m}$

$= \mathrm{Succ}{:}\mathrm{Sum}{:}\langle\overline{m},\overline{n}\rangle$ □

To see how the relator Prod works, we break up its application into three steps.

(1) $\langle\langle X,\overline{\overline{0}}\rangle,\ Y\rangle:\langle\overline{m},\overline{n}\rangle = \langle\langle\overline{m},\overline{0}\rangle,\ \overline{n}\rangle$

(2) In relation to the second step, notice that

$$\langle X,Sum\rangle:\langle\overline{i},\overline{j}\rangle = \langle\overline{i},\overline{i+j}\rangle$$

so that

$\langle X,Sum\rangle\#:\langle\langle\overline{m},\overline{0}\rangle,\ \overline{n}\rangle$

$\quad = \langle X,Sum\rangle^{n}:\langle\overline{m},\overline{0}\rangle$ by 4.2(10)

$\quad = \langle\overline{m},\ \overline{n\cdot m+0}\rangle$

The last line of the proof is abbreviated. A detailed proof would involve the recursive definition of the product function for the integers in terms of the sum function, and would use a method very much like the method used by Hoare [11] for proving the correctness of _while_ loops.

(3) $Prod:\langle\overline{m},\overline{n}\rangle = Y:\langle\overline{m},\ \overline{n\cdot m+0}\rangle = \overline{n\cdot m}$

It is interesting to compare this with the execution of the corresponding Pascal [13] program

```
function prod(m,n: integer): integer;
  var a,j: integer;
  begin
    a := 0;
    for j := 1 to n do
      a := a+m;
    prod := a
  end
```

The term $\langle\langle X,\overline{\overline{0}}\rangle,\ Y\rangle$ in Prod converts the input data structure, $\langle\overline{m},\overline{n}\rangle$, into $\langle\langle\overline{m},\overline{0}\rangle,\ \overline{n}\rangle$. This corresponds to the combined effect of the declaration of the variable a and its initialization; a position is created in which the product can be formed. The term $\langle X,Sum\rangle\#$ corresponds to the _for_ statement, and the final Y to the statement prod:=a combined with the housekeeping operations which occur on exit from the function: irrelevant information is discarded, leaving only the result of the computation.

In defining the relators $\underline{Gt}$ to $\underline{Ne}$ we take advantage of the fact that, by 4.2(7), Prdiff:<$\overline{m}$,$\overline{n}$> is nonzero if and only if m>n. The relators for Quot and Rem can be analysed in much the same way as we analysed Prod.

To conclude this section, I shall give the loop optimization theorem for A# corresponding to Theorems 3.3(13) and 3.3(14). The theorem may be verbalized as follows: if the conditions of 4.2(13) concerning A and B are satisfied, then application of (A·B)# to <x,$\overline{0}$> yields x, while application to <x, $\overline{n}$> for n>0 has the same effect as applying A once to x and then applying B# to the resultant pair <A:x,$\overline{n}$>. (That is to say, the result in this case will be A·B^n:x.)

4.2(13) <u>Theorem (For-loop Optimization)</u>. Let A be an idempotent total function and B a relator such that A·B=A·B·A. Then

(A·B)#:<x,$\overline{n}$> = (Y·Nonzero→<X·A,Y>·B#/X):<x,$\overline{n}$>.

<u>Proof</u>.

Notice that, by Definition 4.2(8),

(A·B)# = (Y·Nonzero ?<X·A·B,Y·Pred>)·X
= (Y·Nonzero ?<X·A,Y>·<X·B,Y·Pred>)·X   by 3.4(4)
= (P?(M·N))·X

where

P = Y·Nonzero,
M = <X·A,Y> and
N = <X·B,Y·Pred>.

We shall be applying Theorem 3.3(13) in the form

P?(M·N) = P→M·(P?N)/I

so that we need to verify that the conditions of that theorem are satisfied.

(i) P and M are deterministic, since A is.

(ii) M·M = <X·A,Y>·<X·A,Y>
= <X·A·A,Y>   by 3.4(4)
= <X·A,Y>   since A is idempotent
= M.

(iii) M•N•M = <X•A,Y>•<X•B,Y•Pred>•<X•A,Y>
= <X•A•B•A,Y•Pred>   by 3.4(4)
= <X•A•B,Y•Pred>   since A•B•A=A•B
= <X•A,Y>•<X•B,Y•Pred>.

(iv) M•P = <X•A,Y>•Y•Nonzero
= Y•Nonzero   since A is total
= P.

Thus
(A•B)# = (P?(M•N))•X
= (P→M•(P?N)/I)•X   by 3.3(13)
= P→M•(P?N)•X/X
= P→M•B#/X
= Y•Nonzero→<X•A,Y>•B#/X   □

4.3 Anomalous Operations

In Section 4.1 we drew a distinction between a proper and a virtual extension of a calculus, and in Section 4.2 we have looked at a virtual extension of RW in some detail. What does the difference between a proper and a virtual extension amount to in practice?

Provided they are applied only to numerals, the numeric operations like Succ, Sum, Prod etc. behave precisely like their integer equivalents - the two are indistinguishable as long as we maintain a rigorous type discipline. But as soon as we relax this discipline, we open the way for what I shall call "anomalous operations", that is to say, operations in relation to the virtual extension which have no counterpart in the proper extension. For example, Nonzero behaves as a predicate, always yielding either t or f, when applied to a numeral; when applied to an arbitrary element of W it may yield any value whatever. Again, Y:$\overline{n}$ gives $\overline{n \dot{-} 1}$ if n>0, but gives f when n=0. If we had introduced the integers into RW by making a proper extension, Nonzero would have been applicable only to integers, while Y would not be applicable to any integer, since the integers would be atoms.

High level languages are often designed with strong typing to exclude anomalous operations. The compiler keeps track of the type of every constant, variable and expression, and reports a type error whenever a mis-match occurs. It might be thought that devices like this belong purely to the world of practical programming, and that they have no place in the more theoretical atmosphere of the relational calculus. But we shall see in the next chapter that they can have quite an important role there too.

Chapter 5. TYPES AND STRUCTURES

In Chapter 4 we saw in general terms what is involved in extending a relational calculus to include a new data type. The example which was given there of extending RW to include the non-negative integers raised the question of anomalous operations. Also, it gave no indication of how we should deal with structured data. This chapter will be devoted mainly to these two questions.

5.1 Dynamic and Static Typing

Suppose we have a programming language with semantics given in terms of an underlying relational calculus; each program in the language is a representation of an expression in the calculus. Then it follows that every data type which exists or can be defined within the language must also be definable within the calculus. And it also follows that any controls on typing that exist within the language like compile-time type checking must be expressible within the calculus. We shall look at typing and type checking as they apply to relational calculi in this section; the application to programming languages will be made in Chapter 7.

The crux of the problem of anomalous operations is that a relator may be applied to an element of an inappropriate type: Nonzero ceases to be a predicate when applied to non-numerals, and Y behaves like the predecessor functions almost, but not quite always. This problem will therefore provide a good starting point for a discussion of types.

One solution that comes to mind is this: set up a calculus on a base set in which every element has the form <type, value>, and ensure that every relator checks that its operands have the correct type. The type component may be drawn from any suitable set - the integers, a set of identifiers, or perhaps from a systematic representation of types like that of Ehrich [9]. This approach to the problem uses dynamic typing, in contrast to the static typing commonly used in programming languages.

There is a second reason for using type checking in programming languages, apart from the need to catch anomalous operations. A number of commonly used operator signs are ambiguous. For example, in many languages we can write "-x" regardless of whether x is real or integer. It is necessary that the type of x be known, so that the right operation can be performed. It should be clear that the dynamically typed relational calculus of the last paragraph can also deal with these "polymorphic" operations adequately. The relator expression will look at the types of its operands, and then select the subexpression appropriate for the types it is dealing with. In fact, anything that can be done with static typing can also be done with a dynamic system like the one proposed; but the converse is not true: there are some things that require dynamic typing (and most experienced programmers know of loopholes in their favorite static language that can be used to get the effect of dynamic typing).

Given that type checking is to be performed in a programming language, static typing is used in preference to dynamic typing for two reasons. Firstly, it enables many errors to be caught at compile time rather than run time, and secondly, it is more efficient. (Obviously it is better to determine the types of x[i] and sum in

<u>for</u> i := 1 <u>to</u> n <u>do</u> sum := sum + x[i]

once and for all at compile time, rather than repeating the determination at each execution of the loop.) So we may ask, if static typing has these advantages for programming languages, are there going to be corresponding disadvantages in using dynamic typing in relational calculi?

The question of catching errors early does not really arise in a relational calculus since it is not its function to supplant the programming languages as a means of expressing algorithms. I shall leave the question of efficiency to Chapter 7, as also the related question of whether a dynamically typed calculus is suitable for defining the semantics of a statically typed language.

On the credit side for dynamic typing, the use of dynamic types will have the effect of producing a useful conceptual factorization of data structures, when we come to deal with them, since it will enable us to separate questions of structure from questions of type. Consider, for example, the following declaration in the statically typed language, Pascal [13].

```
var x: array [1..3] of real;
    r: record
         p: Boolean;
         j: integer;
         c: char
       end
```

From the point of view of types, the array is distinguished from the record by the fact that all its components must have the same type. From the point of view of structures, both the array and the record define a mapping from three fixed elements to a set of values. (This is especially obvious if one considers a dynamic implementation of records in which the field identifiers are retained at run time.) By factoring out and disregarding the question of type, we are able to see a relationship between arrays and records which is otherwise obscured.

5.2 Structured Types

When we come to look at a dynamically typed system in detail, we are immediately faced with the question of whether we are to set up a new relational calculus in which each element of the base set has the form <type, value>, or whether we will use a virtual extension of a simpler calculus to get the desired effect. In Section 5.3 I shall give an example of the latter kind, in which a system implementing a number of types is set up within RW. For the type checking of such a system to be rigorous, it is necessary that it should comprise a complete reproduction of the type-checked calculus, and that the "user" (as distinct from what one might call the "systems programmer" who prepares the reproduction) refrains from using any relator or relational operation from RW. In the interests of simplicity I will relax this rule a little in 5.3 and allow the user access to X, Y and the <A,B> operation.

In dealing with structured types, how are we to map the "value" component of the <type, value> pair into a structured datum - or to put it another way, how are we to represent structures?

The short answer is that we define an Abst function, as given in Definition 4.1(1), to map the set from which the "value" component is drawn into the set of structures. The actual detail of how this is done is entirely dependent on the specifics of the two sets, of course. However, one comment is in order here: just as it is possible to have a two-level system, in which a typed calculus is reproduced within an untyped host calculus, so it is possible to have a stratified multi-level system in which each level is implemented in terms of the levels below it. The example to follow is of this kind.

5.3 An Example: Typed Calculi in RW

Since RW has already been extended to include a set of numerals, the simplest way to represent the type in the pair <type,value> is by a numeral. I will use the symbols Boolean, integer, file and so on to denote the numerals corresponding to the various types, without troubling to fix their values, except for the stipulation that no two may be the same. The constant relators yielding these numerals will be Boolean, integer, file, etc.

Although the main interest of this section is in structures, we cannot avoid introducing typed versions of the Boolean values and the (positive and negative) integers.

5.3(1) Definition. The truth values will be represented by

<Boolean, t> for true, and

<Boolean, f> for false.

Corresponding to these are the constant relators

TRUE = <Boolean, T>, and

FALSE = <Boolean, F>.

Before going further, I shall define an auxiliary relator which will be used for type checking throughout this section.

5.3(2) Definition. Val(type) = <X,type>·Eq→Y/Z

Suppose Val(type1) is applied to an element z of the form <type2,y>. Application of <X,type1> yields <type2,type1> so that

Val(type1):z = y if type1 = type2

is undefined otherwise.

Thus Val(type) gives the value component of its operand pair if the type component is correct, and aborts if it is incorrect.

If type checking is to be strict it is necessary to introduce new type-checked relational operations; these will be used exclusively in place of the original operations, once the system has been set up. As a first example let us define a type-checked version of the conditional, P→A/B.

IF P THEN A ELSE B = P·Val(Boolean)→A/B

If the result of applying P is Boolean, P·Val(Boolean) will yield t or f corresponding to the result, and this is then used to select A or B for application; A and B will have their own internal type checking. If the result of applying P is not Boolean an abort occurs. (I will use keywords composed entirely of capitals to distinguish type-checked operations, except when they are auxiliary "system" operations like Val. The syntax of RW$^+$ does not provide for new notations like IF P THEN A ELSE B; when I use these notations they are understood to be syntactic sugaring for valid RW$^+$ expressions - say IF(P,A,B) in this case.)

We will use WHILE P DO A and REPEAT A UNTIL P for the type checked versions of P?A and A!P. Similarly, there will be type checked versions of and, or etc. For example

P AND Q
 = <P·Val(Boolean), Q·Val(Boolean)> (*)
 ·<Boolean, X and Y>.

If the results of applying P and Q are not both Boolean the calculation aborts at the line marked (*). If they are, this line takes the two values, elements of {t,f}, and puts them together in a pair, so that the and operation can be conveniently performed in the next line. One consequence is that the problem mentioned in connection with and after Definition 2.2(3) does not arise in connection with AND: AND behaves precisely like the normal conjunction operation.

The techniques illustrated in these two examples are also adequate for setting up numeric and other scalar types. In the case of type integer, we need to decide how we are going to represent the negative integers. If efficiency is not required, the neatest way is to use the pair $<\overline{i},\overline{j}>$ of untyped numerals (as defined in 4.2(3)) to represent the integer i-j. For example $<\overline{8},\overline{11}>$ represents -3 while $<\overline{10},\overline{7}>$ represents 3; every integer has infinitely many representations so that all pairs of the form $<\overline{i},\overline{i}>$, for example, represent 0. In addition to the value we must specify the type, of course, so that the element of W representing i-j will be $\langle\overline{\text{integer}},\langle\bar{i},\bar{j}\rangle\rangle$.

To implement, say, subtraction, we notice that

$$(i_1-j_1)-(i_2-j_2) = (i_1+j_2)-(j_1+i_2).$$

Since i_1+j_2 and j_1+i_2 must both be non-negative, the right hand side yields a representation of an integer. We put

$$\begin{aligned}&\text{DIFF}\\ &\quad = \langle X\cdot\text{Val(integer)},\ Y\cdot\text{Val(integer)}\rangle \qquad\qquad (*)\\ &\qquad \cdot\langle\overline{\overline{\text{integer}}},\langle\langle X\cdot X,Y\cdot Y\rangle\cdot\text{Sum},\langle X\cdot Y,Y\cdot X\rangle\cdot\text{Sum}\rangle\rangle.\end{aligned}$$

If the operand of DIFF has the form

$$\langle\langle\overline{\text{integer}},\langle\overline{i_1},\overline{j_1}\rangle\rangle,\ \langle\overline{\text{integer}},\langle\overline{i_2},\overline{j_2}\rangle\rangle\rangle$$

the line (*) yields

$$z = \langle\langle\overline{i_1},\overline{j_1}\rangle,\ \langle\overline{i_2},\overline{j_2}\rangle\rangle$$

so that, in the next line,

$X\cdot X{:}z = \overline{i_1}$,

$X\cdot Y{:}z = \overline{j_1}$,

$Y\cdot X{:}z = \overline{i_2}$ and

$Y\cdot Y{:}z = \overline{j_2}$.

Thus the effect of the second line of the expression for DIFF is to construct an element of the form

$$\langle\overline{\text{integer}},\ \langle\overline{i_1+j_2},\ \overline{j_1+i_2}\rangle\rangle$$

as required.

Notice that the definition of DIFF is independent of the definition of Sum, in the sense that we could replace the latter by a more efficient definition, using binary representation for example, and reap the benefits for DIFF without changing its definition in any way. If we were serious about efficiency, of course, we would also change the representation of negative integers, and therefore DIFF, too; but this is not the point. What is interesting is the fact that in setting up a stratified calculus of the kind proposed in Section 5.2, we can make the higher levels independent of the lower levels in this way. The analogy with the use of procedures to modularize programs should be obvious.

The rationals could be represented in much the same way. For example $\langle\overline{real},\langle\langle\bar{i},\bar{j}\rangle,\bar{k}\rangle\rangle$ could be a representative of $(i-j)/k$ where $i,j \geq 0$ and $k > 0$. The implementation is straightforward but tedious.

All the work in this section, so far, has simply been preparatory to setting up representations of the most common structures: arrays, records and files. However, it turns out to be simpler to define a representation of a stack first and then approach the other types via this, since stacks can be represented in RW in a way which allows all the stack operations to be performed easily and naturally. The same is not true for arrays, for example: if we try to represent arrays directly in terms of binary trees, the assignment operation turns out to be uncomfortably messy.

Before detailing the full implementation of stacks, I shall give a simplified example to bring out the underlying idea. Suppose we wish to represent the stack $x_1,\ldots,x_n$ in which the top element is x_n. Making use of a dummy element d, which is needed to start the stack building process, but which is not part of the stack, we represent the stack by the element

$$s = \langle x_n,\langle x_{n-1},\langle\ldots\langle x_1,d\rangle\ldots\rangle\rangle\rangle.$$

Suppose, now, we wish to replace the top, x_n, by y. The relator $\langle Y,X\cdot Y\rangle$ does this, if the operand is presented to it in the form $\langle s,y\rangle$.

If the reader has any doubts about the "messiness" of assignment to an array, he may like to try the following exercise: assume the s of the last paragraph represents the array $[x_1,\ldots,x_n]$, and devise a relator which, when applied to $\langle\langle s,\bar{i}\rangle,y\rangle$, replaces x_i in this array by y. Any solution of this problem is likely to involve a stack implicitly or explicitly.

Our simplified representation of the stack is inadequate in one respect: it gives us no way of knowing when the stack is empty. The easiest way to provide this facility is to carry the depth of the stack as an untyped numeral, and use the fact that this is zero in an empty stack.

5.3(3) <u>Definition</u>. The stack $x_1,\ldots,x_n$, where x_n is the top, is represented by

$$\langle \overline{\text{stack}},\ \langle \overline{n},\ \langle x_n, \langle \ldots \langle x_1, f\rangle \ldots\rangle\rangle\rangle\rangle;$$

in particular, the empty stack is

$$\langle \overline{\text{stack}},\ \langle \overline{0}, f\rangle\rangle.$$

5.3(4) <u>Definition</u>. The stack operations are

$$\begin{aligned}
&\text{NEWSTACK} = \langle \overline{\overline{\text{stack}}},\ \langle \overline{\overline{0}},\ \text{F}\rangle\rangle,\\
&\text{ISNEW} = \langle \overline{\overline{\text{Boolean}}},\ \langle \text{Val(stack)}\cdot \text{X}, \overline{\overline{0}}\rangle \cdot \text{Eq}\rangle,\\
&\text{PUSH} = \langle \text{X}\cdot \text{Val(stack)}, \text{Y}\rangle\\
&\qquad \cdot \langle \overline{\overline{\text{stack}}},\ \langle \text{X}\cdot \text{X}\cdot \text{Succ}, \langle \text{Y}, \text{X}\cdot \text{Y}\rangle\rangle\rangle,\\
&\text{POP} = \text{Val(stack)}\cdot(\text{X}\cdot \text{Nonzero} \rightarrow \langle \overline{\overline{\text{stack}}}, \langle \text{X}\cdot \text{Pred}, \text{Y}\cdot \text{Y}\rangle\rangle / \text{Z}),\\
&\text{TOP} = \text{Val(stack)}\cdot(\text{X}\cdot \text{Nonzero} \rightarrow \text{Y}\cdot \text{X}/\text{Z}).
\end{aligned}$$

Application of NEWSTACK to any element of W produces an empty stack. PUSH is applicable to a pair <s,y> where s is a stack and y (if the operation is to be legitimate) has the form <type,value>. If the stack has the form given in 5.3(3), the result of <X·Val(stack),Y> is

$$\langle\langle \overline{n},\ \langle x_n, \langle \ldots \langle x_1, f\rangle \ldots\rangle\rangle\rangle,\ y\rangle$$

so that $\langle \overline{\overline{\text{stack}}},\ \langle \text{X}\cdot \text{X}\cdot \text{Succ}, \langle \text{Y}, \text{X}\cdot \text{Y}\rangle\rangle\rangle$ yields

$$\langle \overline{\text{stack}},\ \langle \overline{n+1}, \langle y, \langle x_n, \langle \ldots \langle x_1, f\rangle \ldots\rangle\rangle\rangle\rangle\rangle,$$

as would be expected.

The other three operations all take a stack as operand. If this has the form given in 5.3(3), the result of Val(stack) is, in each case,

$$\langle \overline{n},\ \langle x_n, \langle \ldots \langle x_1, f\rangle \ldots\rangle\rangle\rangle.$$

ISNEW tests for n=0 and constructs a typed Boolean result. POP and TOP are both undefined if n=0. If n>0, POP constructs the stack

$$\langle \overline{\text{stack}},\ \langle \overline{n-1},\ \langle x_{n-1}, \langle \ldots \langle x_1, f\rangle \ldots\rangle\rangle\rangle\rangle$$

while TOP returns x_n.

5. Types and Structures

The informal kind of semantic specification that I have been using is adequate for many purposes. There are times, though, when a more rigorous approach is needed.

When we set up our representation of the non-negative integers, we proved correctness by reference to Peano's Postulates. Similarly, if an abstract data type can be defined by means of a set of axioms, these axioms can be used to check the correctness of a representation of the type. It would be premature to go at all deeply into this subject here, since it is still an area of vigorous research at the present time. However, it will be useful to show how our stack operations are related to a treatment of stacks in a paper by Guttag, Horowitz and Musser [10]. They give a set of axioms for an abstract data type, Stack, and then show how to prove correctness for an implementation in terms of type Array, also specified by axioms. I will show how a similar proof could be constructed in our system - although our axioms for an abstract stack would differ slightly from theirs, since they specify that application of POP to an empty stack yields an empty stack, where we say that POP is not applicable.

There are six axioms for the abstract data type, Stack. Corresponding to these we must have, for every element s of type stack and y of arbitrary type,

(1) NEWSTACK•POP = Z,

(2) NEWSTACK•TOP = Z,

(3) NEWSTACK•ISNEW = TRUE,

(4) PUSH•POP:<s,y> = s,

(5) PUSH•TOP:<s,y> = y, and

(6) PUSH•ISNEW:<s,y> = $\overline{\langle \text{Boolean,f} \rangle}$.

As an example, I will show how (5) may be verified. Refer to 5.3(4), first of all, to see that PUSH•TOP can be written as A•B•C•D where

```
     A = <X·Val(stack), Y>,
     B = <stack, <X·X·Succ, <Y,X·Y>>>,
     C = Val(stack),
     D = X·Nonzero→Y·X/Z.
Let s = <stack, <n,z>>. Then
A·B·C·D:<s,y>
     = B·C·D:<<n,z>, y>
     = C·D:<stack, <n+1, <y,z>>>
     = D:<n+1, <y,z>>
     = y     since n+1≠0.
```

The definition of sequential files in terms of stacks is a simple matter. Since operations can only take place in the immediate neighbourhood of the read-write head, one may represent the parts of the file before and after the head by two stacks, each with its top adjacent to the head. A movement of the head involves popping one stack and pushing its top on the other stack.

I will use the notation $[x_1,\ldots,x_{j-1}|x_j,\ldots,x_n]$ for a file in which the head is positioned between elements x_{j-1} and x_j. Thus $[|x_1,\ldots,x_n]$ will denote a rewound file, $[x_1,\ldots,x_n|]$ a file in end-of-file condition, and $[|]$ an empty file.

5.3(5) Definition.

```
NEWFILE = <file, <NEWSTACK, NEWSTACK> >
READ = Val(file)·<<file,<<X,Y·TOP>·PUSH,Y·POP>>, Y·TOP>
LOOK = Val(file)·Y·TOP
EOF = Val(file)·Y·ISNEW
WRITE = <X·Val(file),Y>
          ·(IF X·Y·ISNEW
              THEN <file,<<X·X,Y>·PUSH,X·Y>>
              ELSE <file,<<X·X,Y>·PUSH,X·Y·POP>>)
```

```
REWIND = Val(file)
            •(WHILE NOT X•ISNEW DO
                <X•POP,<Y,X•TOP>•PUSH>)
            •<file,I>
```

For every x in W, NEWFILE:x = [|]. As can be seen from the expression for NEWFILE, the empty file will be represented by

$$\langle \underline{\text{file}}, \langle\langle \underline{\text{stack}}, \langle \bar{0}, f\rangle\rangle, \langle \underline{\text{stack}}, \langle \bar{0}, f\rangle\rangle\rangle\rangle.$$

The representation could be changed to omit the two type flags "stack", which, after all, could be taken to be implied by the flag "file". However, this slight gain in the elegance of the representation would be paid for by a considerable increase in the complexity of the implementations in 5.3(5).

In commenting on the other file relators I shall assume that $z = [x_1,\ldots,x_{j-1}|x_j,\ldots,x_n]$. Then we have

$$\text{READ}:z = \langle [x_1,\ldots,x_j|x_{j+1},\ldots,x_n], x_j\rangle.$$

Thus READ•Y gives x_j, the element to the right of the read-write head before the READ operation was performed, while READ•X gives the file z unchanged except that the head has moved one place right. The presence of Y•TOP and Y•POP in the expression for READ means that READ is not applicable to a file in end-of-file condition.

LOOK:z yields x_j if z is not in end-of-file condition; otherwise LOOK is not applicable.

EOF:z yields the (typed) value true if z is in end-of-file condition, and false otherwise. WRITE differs from the usual write operation for a sequential file, in that it acts as a replacement operator if z is not in end-of-file condition. (This facilitates the definition of ASSIGN.) Thus,

$$\begin{aligned} \text{WRITE}:\langle z,y\rangle &= [x_1,\ldots,x_{j-1},y|x_{j+1},\ldots,x_n] \text{ if } j\leq n, \\ &= [x_1,\ldots,x_n,y|] \text{ if } j=n+1. \end{aligned}$$

As would be expected, REWIND:z = $[|x_1,\ldots,x_n]$.

To conclude this section, I shall define a structured type "table". This may be described by comparing it to a conventional array type, for example the type defined by

<u>array</u> [-50..50] <u>of</u> real

in Pascal [13]. This is in fact a mapping from a finite set of contiguous integers into the reals. A table, by contrast, is a mapping from a finite set of integers, which need not be contiguous, into elements of arbitrary type, not necessarily all the same. Clearly, a normal array is a special case of a table, as is a sparse array. But also, a record can very easily be represented as a table; all that is necessary is to define a one-one mapping of the identifiers into the integers, so that each field identifier is replaced by a unique integer.

Suppose the table consists of the pairs $<u_1,v_1>,\ldots,<u_n,v_n>$, where $u_1,\ldots,u_n$ are distinct integers and $v_1,\ldots,v_n$ are the corresponding table values. Then we will denote this table by $[u_1:v_1,\ldots,u_n:v_n]$ and represent it in RW by a file in which these pairs are the components, and occur in the same order.

5.3(6) <u>Definition</u>

```
NEWTABLE = <table,NEWFILE>
Locate = <X·Val(table)·REWIND, Y>
         ·(WHILE
             (IF X·EOF THEN FALSE ELSE <X·LOOK·X, Y>·NE)
           DO <X·READ·X, Y>)
         ·X
ACCESS = Locate·LOOK·Y
ASSIGN = <table,<X·Locate, <X·Y,Y>>·WRITE>
```

NEWTABLE:x produces an empty table for any x in W, that is to say, it produces the element <table, [|]>.

Suppose z is the table $[u_1:v_1,\ldots,u_n:v_n]$. Then Locate:<z,j>, where j is an element of type integer, yields the file

$$[<u_1,v_1>,\ldots|<u_k,v_k>,\ldots,<u_n,v_n>]$$

where k is the smallest integer for which u_k=j. If there is no

u_k=j, the file is returned in end-of-file condition. This is an ancilliary relator, only defined for use in ACCESS and ASSIGN. In Locate, NE is the test for inequality of two elements of type integer.

With the same value of z, ACCESS:<z,j> yields v_k, where k is defined as before; ACCESS:<z,j> is undefined if no u_k=j. ASSIGN:<<z,j>,y> returns a new table in which the pair <u_k,v_k> found by Locate is replaced by <j,y>; when no u_k=j, a new pair <j,y> is appended to the end of the table. Apart from the point just noted, these are the familiar access and assign operations.

5.4 Mathematical Models

To conclude this chapter and lead into the next, I shall point out connections and parallels which exist between the work we have been doing and mathematical modelling.

Imagine as elementary physics exercise aimed at getting students to verify Hooke's Law, and to construct a spring balance. The instructions might run as follows: Suspend a spring with a pointer moving on a scale and a pan attached to the bottom end. Measure the displacement with a number of known weights in the pan, and graph displacement against weight. What is the relation between them? Use the device to weigh (say) a textbook.

The first point to notice is that the set of instructions just given defines a mapping from one state of the physical system to a pair of real numbers, <mass, displacement>. Many other mappings are possible: students might be asked to note the dimensions of the object in the pan, the period of oscillation, the time of day, or the temperature, for example. In this respect, the observational process corresponds to what I called "abstraction" in Section 4.1, with the system in a particular state serving as "representation" and the observational data as abstraction. Just as there are many observations that can be carried out on a physical system, so there are many mappings that can be applied to strings, say, of digits; "101", for example, may be interpreted as a binary numeral, a character string of length 3, a string for which the assertion "This is a palindrome" is true, and so on. In both cases, one of many possible functions is chosen to map the "representation" set into the abstraction set; but of course, in the context of experimentation, the term "representation" is no longer appropriate to describe a state of an experimental system.

The students are to make a number of observations on the system and mark their results as points on a graph. This set of points can be regarded as a finite dyadic relation on the real numbers; I shall call it E. If a student draws a line passing through all the points of E, he has defined another relation, H, such that $E \subset H$.

If the only information available about the behaviour of the spring is contained in the relation E, then H must be regarded as hypothetical; it is not uniquely determined by $E \subset H$. Any number of curves can be drawn passing through a given finite set of points. This is an illustration of the well known problem in the philosophy of science: while a theory may certainly be disproved by experimental data, it is not at all clear how it can ever be proved. However, the chances are that the student will ignore the scope for creativity given in the instructions, and put a straight line through his points, finishing up with some statement such as, "d=25.3m, where d is the displacement in centimetres and m the mass in kilograms."

Leaving aside questions of philosophy, then, we may say that both the graph and the formula d=25.3m are descriptions of the system - or rather, because of their hypothetical character, we should say they are purported descriptions. Just as the pair <.36,9.1> describes one state of the system from the point of view of the mass-displacement abstraction, so d=25.3m purports to describe all its states from the same point of view. And the important thing to notice is that this formula may be regarded as a relator in a suitable relational calculus.

The remark just made is applicable not only to simple systems like the spring balance. Any system at all for which there is a mathematical model giving one aspect of the system explicitly in terms of others is amenable to the same treatment: a relator expression can be given which is the purported description of the system, encapsulating a hypothesis about it.

Much of the work of a scientist using a computer amounts to formulating a hypothesis as a program and then using the computer to test if it is compatible with observed data, to evaluate the parameters of the model, and finally, using it to make predictions. Since the program is a representation of a relator expression, all these activities can be viewed as implicit applications of the point made in the last paragraph. Nevertheless, it would be better if the applications were made with an explicit understanding, for, just as the formulation of a hypothesis in mathematical terms enables us to use the resources of mathematics, so its formulation as a relator expression may enable us to use the additional resources of a relational calculus. Once we have given the force required to extend a spring through a known distance as a mathematical expression we may, for example, integrate to find the energy stored in the extended spring; and once we express a more complex hypothesis as a relator, we may hope to apply theorems like those of Chapter 3 to get new results.

There are two other things to notice. Firstly, it is because the objects which are being described are complex, made up of other objects, and each having many degrees of freedom, that we need data structures like those considered in this chapter. Not only do we need to be able to use a number of scalar variables to specify the degrees of freedom - we also need to be able to structure our data to mirror the structure of the object.

5. Types and Structures

If a structured datum gives a snapshot of one state of the system, then the relator expression corresponding to the hypothesis gives a comprehensive description of a whole range of states. Thus the second point is this: it is because the behaviour of the system is regular and not chaotic that we may use an expression in a relator calculus to describe it. The structure of this expression should manifest the regularities of the behaviour of the system.

Chapter 6. PROGRAMS

The statement was made in the Introduction, and again at the end of the last chapter, that a program is a representation of a relator. In this chapter we shall explore some of the implications of this statement, using the notions of representation and implementation introduced in Definitions 4.1(1) and 4.1(2). But before doing this, it is worth noticing that we have recently been dealing with another kind of representation of a relator - or rather, of a relation, which amounts to the same thing.

The data type, table, of 5.3(6) is a set of pairs, that is, a dyadic relation. The first element of each pair is of integer type (mainly to make sure that the inequality test, NE, is available for Locate) and the second an arbitrary typed element. However, these typing restrictions could easily be relaxed, to allow for the representation of any finite relation. So we may ask, Why do we sometimes represent a relation (or relator) in tabular form and sometimes by a program?

Often it is a simple economic question of striking a balance between execution time and memory requirement. If a calculation used the squares of the integers from 1 to 1000 in an unpredictable order and with repetitions, we would evaluate them each time by multiplication, but if it used the first thousand primes in the same way we would probably store them in a table at the start of the calculation. It would waste space to store the squares, whereas it would waste time to recompute the primes.

These are essentially economic factors. But as I pointed out at the end of the last chapter, there is another more fundamental factor, namely intelligibility. Some aspects of a system are most clearly described by a data structure, others by a program, others again by a hybrid like an array of functions or an array valued function.

6.1 Semantics

The set of relators on a base set S is given by Rel(S) = $\{R | R \subseteq S^2\}$. If S is countably infinite Rel(S) is non-countable, and, in general, whatever the cardinality of S, the cardinality of Rel(S) is higher, so that there can never be a function from S onto Rel(S). In terms of Definition 4.1(1), this means that we can never have a total representation of Rel(S) in S - there will always be relators in Rel(S) which are not represented. However, the existence of non-computable relators is a basic fact of computational life, and it would be pointless to try to circumvent it by taking a set larger than the base set as the set of programs, so I will assume that all programs are elements of the base set; if necessary, the calculus will be extended to include them.

The assertion that every program is a representation of a relator can now be made more specific.

6.1(1) Thesis. Corresponding to every programming language in which programs and data are drawn from the set S, there is a function Sem:$S \rightarrow$Rel(S) such that, for every program p in the language, the relator Sem(p) gives the effect of executing p. Sem is called the semantic function of the language.

The use of "semantic function" here (or "semantics" for short) agrees with the current usage of the computing community. The semantics of a language is, precisely, a specification which allows one to infer what function or relator is defined by each program in the language.

Programs need not be character strings; machine language programs are not, for example. But when they are strings, I shall adopt the practice of denotational semantics and write Sem⟦p⟧ rather than Sem(p). This is to be taken as an indication that the string-valued variables and constants within the hollow brackets are to be concatenated to give a single string.

Since 6.1(1) is an application of the idea of representation introduced in 4.1(1), it is reasonable to ask whether we can also make use of the "implementation" of 4.1(2). Although that definition was restricted to the implementations of dyadic relators, the underlying idea can easily be extended to more general cases. Thus we ask, Are there any functions or relations on the set of relators Rel(S) which we might wish to implement in the set of programs representing Rel(S)?

If we refer back to Chapter 1, we see that the relational operations are in fact functions of the form $F:Rel(S)^n \rightarrow Rel(S)$. For example, corresponding to the composition operation of 1.2(1) is the function $Comp:Rel(S)^2 \rightarrow Rel(S)$ with $Comp(A,B)=A \cdot B$ for all relators A and B. All the relational operations can be re-written in this way. Also, the primitive relators are constant functions of the same type, that is, functions for which $n=0$.

6.1(2) <u>Corollary</u> (to 4.1(2)). Let $F:Rel(S)^n \rightarrow Rel(S)$ be a relational operation or primitive relator on the base set S. Then $f:S^n \rightarrow S$ implements F if, for all $p_1,\ldots,p_n$ in S,

$$Sem(f(p_1,\ldots,p_n)) = F(Sem(p_1),\ldots,Sem(p_n)).$$

The function f which implements F will be called the <u>program constructor</u> corresponding to F.

This kind of implementation is rather different from the implementations we have encountered in Chapters 4 and 5. Before thinking about these differences, it will be useful to look at one or two examples.

6.1(3) <u>Example</u>. Assume that RW has been extended to include character strings. Then a programming language could be set up in RW having the semantic function Sem defined recursively by

$$\mathrm{Sem}[\![\underline{\mathrm{true}}]\!] = \mathrm{T}$$

$$\mathrm{Sem}[\![\underline{\mathrm{false}}]\!] = \mathrm{F}$$

$$\mathrm{Sem}[\![\underline{\mathrm{x}}]\!] = \mathrm{X}$$

$$\mathrm{Sem}[\![\underline{\mathrm{y}}]\!] = \mathrm{Y}$$

$$\mathrm{Sem}[\![\mathrm{a};\mathrm{b}]\!] = \mathrm{Sem}[\![\mathrm{a}]\!]\cdot\mathrm{Sem}[\![\mathrm{b}]\!]$$

$$\mathrm{Sem}[\![\underline{\mathrm{if}}\ \mathrm{p}\ \underline{\mathrm{then}}\ \mathrm{a}\ \underline{\mathrm{else}}\ \mathrm{b}]\!] = \mathrm{Sem}[\![\mathrm{p}]\!] \rightarrow \mathrm{Sem}[\![\mathrm{a}]\!]\ /\ \mathrm{Sem}[\![\mathrm{b}]\!]$$

$$\mathrm{Sem}[\![\underline{\mathrm{while}}\ \mathrm{p}\ \underline{\mathrm{do}}\ \mathrm{a}]\!] = \mathrm{Sem}[\![\mathrm{p}]\!]\ ?\ \mathrm{Sem}[\![\mathrm{a}]\!]$$

$$\mathrm{Sem}[\![(\mathrm{a},\mathrm{b})]\!] = \langle \mathrm{Sem}[\![\mathrm{a}]\!]\ ,\ \mathrm{Sem}[\![\mathrm{b}]\!]\rangle$$

$$\mathrm{Sem}[\![(\mathrm{a})]\!] = \mathrm{Sem}[\![\mathrm{a}]\!].$$

In this example, p, a and b are arbitrary programs while <u>true</u>, <u>false</u> etc. are constant strings which appear in the program (without underlines; I shall use underlines only when necessary to distinguish string-valued constants from string-valued variables). The four strings, "true", "false", "x" and "y" are regarded as being results of applying four program constructors of the type $W^0 \rightarrow W$. These functions implement the four primitive relators T, F, X and Y, which are likewise regarded as the results of constant functions of type $\mathrm{Rel}(W)^0 \rightarrow \mathrm{Rel}(W)$.

In the fifth semantic equation, the right hand side can be rewritten as Comp(Sem⟦a⟧,Sem⟦b⟧), using the function Comp defined earlier in this section. Suppose we also define a program constructor comp:$W^2 \rightarrow W$ such that comp(a,b), for strings a and b, is the string obtained by concatenating a and b with ";" inserted between them. Then the equation becomes

$$\mathrm{Sem}[\![\mathrm{comp}(\mathrm{a},\mathrm{b})]\!] = \mathrm{Comp}(\mathrm{Sem}[\![\mathrm{a}]\!],\mathrm{Sem}[\![\mathrm{b}]\!]),$$

which is exactly the form of 6.1(2). It should be clear that the other three relational operations can be treated in the same way. In the eighth equation I have used "(a,b)" to avoid confusion with "<a,b>" which, of course, is not a single string but a pair of strings.

In this language, the program representing, say, the relator expression <T, X?Y> would be

(true, while x do y).

We next look at another language for RW in which programs are not strings but trees with numerals as terminal nodes.

6.1(4) Example. The semantic function, Sem, of this language is defined recursively by

$$\mathrm{Sem}(\langle\overline{0},\overline{0}\rangle) = T$$
$$\mathrm{Sem}(\langle\overline{0},\overline{1}\rangle) = F$$
$$\mathrm{Sem}(\langle\overline{0},\overline{2}\rangle) = X$$
$$\mathrm{Sem}(\langle\overline{0},\overline{3}\rangle) = Y$$
$$\mathrm{Sem}(\langle\overline{1},\langle a,b\rangle\rangle) = \mathrm{Sem}(a)\cdot\mathrm{Sem}(b)$$
$$\mathrm{Sem}(\langle\overline{2},\langle p,\langle a,b\rangle\rangle\rangle) = \mathrm{Sem}(p) \rightarrow \mathrm{Sem}(a) \;/\; \mathrm{Sem}(b)$$
$$\mathrm{Sem}(\langle\overline{3},\langle p,a\rangle\rangle) = \mathrm{Sem}(p) \;?\; \mathrm{Sem}(a)$$
$$\mathrm{Sem}(\langle\overline{4},\langle a,b\rangle\rangle) = \langle\mathrm{Sem}(a),\ \mathrm{Sem}(b)\rangle.$$

The analysis here is very similar to that for 6.1(3). In the fifth equation, for example, the program constructor comp satisfies

$$\mathrm{comp}(a,b) = \langle\overline{1},\langle a,b\rangle\rangle.$$

In this language, the program for <T, X?Y> would be

$$\langle\overline{4},\langle\langle\overline{0},\overline{0}\rangle,\langle\overline{3},\langle\langle\overline{0},\overline{2}\rangle,\langle\overline{0},\overline{3}\rangle\rangle\rangle\rangle\rangle.$$

Up to now, I have been speaking of a program constructor "implementing" a primitive relator or relational operation because the relationship is formally the same as that given in 4.1(2). However, the term is not really appropriate. When we say that Succ implements Peano's successor function we mean that Succ may be applied to a numeral to find the successor of the corresponding integer: we can use Succ: $\overline{n}$ to evaluate n'. But there is no suggestion that writing "a;b" somehow enables us to evaluate Sem[[a]]·Sem[[b]] to a single relator. Rather, the purpose of these "implementations" is to define the semantic function, Sem. Thus, I will speak of equation like those used in 6.1(3) and 6.1(4) simply as "semantic equations". The rest of this section is concerned with establishing conditions under which a set of semantic equations does specify a language.

6.1(5) Theorem. Suppose the primitive relators and relational operations of a relational calculus on the base set S are $F_1^{(n_1)}, F_2^{(n_2)}, \ldots$, where

$$F_j^{(n_j)}: Rel(S)^{n_j} \rightarrow Rel(S),$$

and that the semantic function, Sem, of a programming language is defined in terms of the program constructors $f_1^{(n_1)}, f_2^{(n_2)}, \ldots$ by

$$Sem(f_j^{(n_j)}(p_1,\ldots,p_{n_j})) = F_j^{(n_j)}(Sem(p_1),\ldots,Sem(p_{n_j})) \quad (*)$$

for all relevant j and all $p_1,\ldots,p_{n_j}$ in S. Then, if E is any expression formed by composition of the program constructors, Sem(E) is obtained by replacing each $f_j^{(n_j)}$ in E by $F_j^{(n_j)}$.

Proof. The expression E may be regarded as a tree in which each node is a function, $f_j^{(n_j)}(p_1,\ldots,p_{n_j})$, with the expressions $p_1,\ldots,p_{n_j}$ as subnodes. The theorem is proved by structural induction on this tree.

The terminal nodes of the tree are all program constructors corresponding to primitive relators; that is, they have the form $f_j^{(0)}$. For these, we have $Sem(f_j^{(0)})=F_j^{(0)}$, so that the assertion of the theorem is true for any tree consisting of a single node.

Consider any non-terminal node $f_j^{(n_j)}(p_1,\ldots,p_{n_j})$, and assume as induction hypothesis that each argument p_k is transformed into $Sem(p_k)$ by replacing each f within it by the corresponding F. Then the effect of performing this replacement on $f_j^{(n_j)}(p_1,\ldots,p_{n_j})$ is to give $F_j^{(n_j)}(Sem(p_1),\ldots,Sem(p_{n_j}))$, which is equal to $Sem(f_j^{(n_j)}(p_1,\ldots,p_{n_j}))$ by the semantic equation (*). □

To see how this replacement process works, let us return to Example 6.1(3). We will convert our notation to functional form by writing

$f_0 = \underline{\text{true}}$	$F_0 = T$
$f_1 = \underline{\text{false}}$	$F_1 = F$
$f_2 = \underline{x}$	$F_2 = X$
$f_3 = \underline{y}$	$F_3 = Y$
$f_4(a,b) = a;b$	$F_4(A,B) = A \cdot B$
$f_5(p,a,b) = \underline{\text{if}}\ p\ \underline{\text{then}}\ a\ \underline{\text{else}}\ b$	$F_5(P,A,B) = P \to A/B$
$f_6(p,a) = \underline{\text{while}}\ p\ \underline{\text{do}}\ a$	$F_6(P,A) = P?A$
$f_7(a,b) = (a,b)$	$F_7(A,B) = <A,B>$
$f_8(a) = (a)$	$F_8(A) = A$

where, for example, a;b means that the strings a and b are concatenated with ";" inserted between them. A program like

if (x;y) then (while y do x) else f

can be rewritten as

$$f_5(f_4(f_2,f_3),f_6(f_3,f_2),f_1).$$

Performing the transformation specified in Theorem 6.1(5) on this results in

$$F_5(F_4(F_2,F_3),F_6(F_3,F_2),F_1)$$

which, in turn, can be rewritten in the RW notation as

$$X \cdot Y \to (Y?X)/F.$$

In applying Theorem 6.1(5) it is necessary to take account of the possibility that two different expressions in the program constructors may evaluate to the same program - in other words, that the set of program constructors, regarded as defining a grammar, is ambiguous. This is, in fact, the case with the language of 6.1(3) which was used in the example above, since we cannot tell whether a;b;c should be $f_4(a,f_4(b,c))$ or $f_4(f_4(a,b),c)$. In this case it does not matter, as it happens, since the associativity of composition means that $F_4(A,F_4(B,C)) = F_4(F_4(A,B),C)$. But in general, the effect of an ambiguity will be that there are several relators corresponding to program, so that the mapping from program to relator is not a function. In terms of the Thesis 6.1(1), this means that the semantic equations do not define a language.

The management of ambiguity is reasonably well understood for languages in which programs are character strings. (The ambiguity just mentioned could be resolved by supplementing 6.1(3) with a syntax including the formula

composition ::= statement | composition ; statement

which has the effect of specifying the direction in which ";" associates.) The ideas of "grammar" and "ambiguity" as applied to objects which are not character strings are less familiar and well understood, although they are straightforward generalizations of the string grammars.

Suppose p=E, where E is an expression in the program constructors and the program p is, as always, an element of the base set. Then if we express E as the tree in which each node is a function, and its subnodes are the arguments of this function in E, the result can be regarded as the <u>parse tree</u> for E. (This was done in the proof of Theorem 6.1(5).)

6.1(6) <u>Definition</u>. The <u>formal language</u> generated by a set of program constructors is

$\{p \mid p=E$ and E is an expression in the program constructors$\}$.

6.1(7) <u>Definition</u>. A set of program constructors is <u>unambiguous</u> if, for any two expressions E_1 and E_2 in the program constructors, $E_1=E_2$ implies that E_1 and E_2 have identical parse trees.

6.1(8) <u>Theorem</u>. A necessary and sufficient condition for a set of program constructors $f_1^{(n_1)}, f_2^{(n_2)}, \ldots$ to be unambiguous is that, in all cases,

$$f_j^{(n_j)}(p_1,\ldots,p_{n_j}) = f_k^{(n_k)}(q_1,\ldots,q_{n_k})$$

implies $j=k$ and $p_i=q_i$ for $i=1,\ldots,n_j$.

<u>Proof</u>.

Necessity: Any instance in which the condition is false constitutes an ambiguity.

Sufficiency: Let E_1 and E_2 be two expressions in the program constructors with $E_1=E_2$. Then we can write

$$E_1 = f_j^{(n_j)}(p_1,\ldots,p_{n_j}) \text{ and}$$
$$E_2 = f_k^{(n_k)}(q_1,\ldots,q_{n_k}),$$

so that $j=k$ and $p_i=q_i$ for all $i \leq n_j$. We can now apply the same reasoning to each pair of subexpressions, and, since the depth of nesting is finite, we may conclude that the parse trees of E_1 and E_2 are identical. □

6.1(9) <u>Definition</u>. A set of semantic equations for a language representing a relator calculus is said to be <u>complete</u> if

(i) there is a program constructor corresponding to each primitive relator and relational operation of the calculus;

(ii) the semantic equations satisfy the conditions (*) of Theorem 6.1(5); and

(iii) the set of program constructors is unambiguous.

6.1(10) <u>Theorem</u>. A complete set of semantic equations defines a programming language for a calculus in which every relator definable by a non-recursive expression in the calculus is represented by a program.

<u>Proof</u>. Since the set of program constructors is unambiguous, there is one parse tree corresponding to each program. The transformation specified in Theorem 6.1(5) maps this into a unique relator, which is the relator defined by the program. This mapping from program to relator defines the language.

The transformation of 6.1(5) can be inverted by replacing each F by the corresponding f. Thus, if there are program constructors for all the primitive relators and relational operations of the calculus, any non-recursive expression in the calculus can be mapped into an expression in the program constructors; the value of this is the program representing the relator. □

The semantic equations of Example 6.1(4) illustrate this theorem. The strategic placing of numerals in these equations ensures that program constructors are unambiguous. Thus, by the theorem the eight equations of 6.1(4) define a language, and any expression in T, F, X, Y and the four relational operations of 2.2(4)(ii) is represented by a program in the language of 6.1(4). And since any expression in RW can be reduced to an expression in these eight primitive relators and relational operations, it follows that the language is adequate for the representation of all the relators definable in RW.

6.2 Semantic Specification Systems

This subject has been dealt with in a paper by Blikle [4], in which he used a relational calculus to study the relationships between several program verification methods. The discussion here will therefore be restricted to a few comments on denotational semantics, an area which he touched on only very lightly. (Also, Section 6.4 is relevant to operational semantics.)

The technique of using systems of equations like those of Example 6.1(3) to specify the semantics of a language is the pivotal idea of denotational semantics; the previous section may be seen as a justification of this technique from the point of view of a relational theory of computing. Nevertheless, if we compare 6.1(3) with the way in which these systems of equations are used in references [19,25,29] for example, we soon notice differences.

These differences are largely attributable to the use by the previous authors of the lambda calculus as a vehicle for the specification of functions. In the first place, this makes it necessary to have a reflexive domain as the domain of data elements, if one is not to risk producing a logically inconsistent system. And, secondly, it tends to introduce a bias towards concepts and definitions that go well with the lambda calculus, so that, for example, recursion is used rather than iteration in specifying the semantics of <u>while</u>. The use of a relational calculus instead of the lambda calculus gives more room to manoeuvre in both respects. There is no danger of producing a paradox in a relational calculus, since relators are not self-applicable; and, for the second point, the operations provided in the relational calculus can be as close as we wish to those of a programming language.

Another difference, which will emerge in Chapter 7, where I define a simple, fairly conventional programming language based on RW, concerns the handling of identifiers occurring in a language. In Strachey's system, the values of identifiers are embodied in an "environment", which is a function mapping each identifier into its value. I will incorporate them, instead, in a global data structure which the relators operate on. In this case, the decision to go one way or the other is largely determined by the need to produce a coherent and aesthetically satisfying system.

6.3 Equivalence of Programs

6.3(1) <u>Definition</u>. Let a and b be two programs in a programming language with semantic function Sem. Then if Sem(a) = Sem(b), we say that a and b are <u>equivalent</u>, and write $a \equiv b$.

To see how an equivalence proof goes when the semantics of a language are specified in terms of relators, let us take the loop optimization theorem, 3.3(13), and transfer it into the language of Example 6.1(3). (I am assuming that the semantic equations of that language have been supplemented with a syntax to remove the ambiguity involving ";".)

Theorem 3.3(13) states that if

(i) P and A are deterministic,

(ii) $A \cdot A = A$,

(iii) $A\cdot P = P$,

(iv) $A\cdot B\cdot A = A\cdot B$.

then $P?(A\cdot B) = P\rightarrow A\cdot(P?B)/I$. Let p, a and b be programs with $Sem[\![p]\!]=P$, $Sem[\![a]\!]=A$ and $Sem[\![b]\!]=B$. Then, since all relators definable in RW are deterministic, (i) is automatically satisfied.

Condition (ii) is rewritten as $Sem[\![a]\!]\cdot Sem[\![a]\!] = Sem[\![a]\!]$, which is satisfied if $Sem[\![a;a]\!] = Sem[\![a]\!]$. In the notation of 6.3(1), this is $a;a\equiv a$. Conditions (iii) and (iv) are treated in the same way.

Theorem 3.3(12) involves a conditional of the form $P\rightarrow C/I$. I will assume that the language has been extended so that the usual _if then_ notation is available:

$$Sem[\![\underline{if}\ p\ \underline{then}\ a]\!] = Sem[\![p]\!]\rightarrow Sem[\![a]\!]/I.$$

Then we have

6.3(2) _Theorem_. If p, a and b are programs in the language of 6.1(3), and

(i) $a;a \equiv a$,

(ii) $a;p \equiv p$,

(iii) $a;b;a \equiv a;b$.

then

$$\underline{while}\ p\ \underline{do}\ (a;b) \equiv \underline{if}\ p\ \underline{then}\ (a;\ \underline{while}\ p\ \underline{do}\ b).$$

Proof. Convert both sides of the asserted equivalence to relators by means of Theorem 6.1(5). Falsity of the equivalence would imply falsity of 3.3(13). □

It is clear that all the theorems of Chapter 3 which assert equality of relators could be treated in the same way. Also, a result like Corollary 3.2(9)(i),

$$P\rightarrow A/Z\subseteq A,$$

would translate into, "If the program '_if_ p _then_ a _else_ _abort_' terminates, it has the same effect as the program a", where _abort_ is defined by $Sem[\![\underline{abort}]\!]=Z$.

The advantage of proving equivalence theorems for relator expressions, rather than directly for programs, is that once a theorem has been proved the result can easily be applied to a great many languages.

6.4 Interpreters

So far in this chapter I have been using semantic equations to define the semantics of a programming language. These equations are external to the relational calculus which is being represented; there is therefore some interest in looking for a method of semantic specification which works entirely within the calculus. In this section I shall show how the familiar idea of an interpreter can be used for this purpose. The material in the section stands in much the same relation to operational semantics as that of Section 6.1 did to denotational semantics.

6.4(1) Definition. Let S be a base set closed under the formation of pairs. Then a relator M on S is an interpreter for a language with semantic function Sem:S→Rel(S) if and only if

$$(\forall p)(\forall x)(\forall y)(\langle p,x\rangle My \iff x\,Sem(p)\,y).$$

This means that the effect of applying M to <p,x> is the same as the effect of applying Sem(p) to x. Notice that M is not completely specified in terms of Sem - there is no indication of the effect of applying M to an atomic element of S.

6.4(2) Definition. An interpreter M is a minimal interpreter if

$$(\forall x)(\forall y)(x \text{ is atomic} \Longrightarrow \sim xMy)$$

(so that M is only applicable to pairs).

The minimal interpreter is the intersection of all the interpreters associated with a semantic function, and is uniquely defined by it. Also, it is clear from 6.4(1) that any interpreter, minimal or otherwise, defines a unique semantic function. Thus we have

6.4(3) *Corollary*. There is exactly one minimal interpreter corresponding to each semantic function, and conversely.

6.4(4) *Notation*. The *relator defined by program p in the interpreter M* is denoted by M{p}, where

$$(\forall x)(\forall y)(x\,M\{p\}\,y \iff \langle p,x\rangle\,M\,y).$$

In all cases M{p} = Sem(p) where Sem is the semantic function corresponding to M. The justification for this addtional notation is that it allows us to specify the relator defined by a program without having to bring in the semantic function.

Because of the parallel between M{p} and Sem(p), everything that was said concerning sets of semantic equations in Section 6.1 can be equally well applied to interpreters. For example, a *non-procedural* definition of an interpreter for the language of 6.1(4) could be given by replacing Sem(...) by M{...} throughout the eight semantic equations:

$$M\{\langle\overline{0},\overline{0}\rangle\} = T,$$

$$\cdot \quad \cdot \quad \cdot \quad \cdot \quad ,$$

$$M\{\langle\overline{4},\langle a,b\rangle\rangle\} = \langle M\{a\}, M\{b\}\rangle.$$

In Section 8.1 I shall give a *procedural* definition for a this language, that is, I shall give a relator expression for M which satisfies this set of equations. Such an expression is equivalent, in our system, to the operational semantics of the language.

Since most people working in computing have a fairly clear idea of what they mean by the terms "language" and "interpreter", it is worth pointing out that the sense they have been given here is very general. According to 6.4(1) an interpreter can be any relator on S. There is no requirement that the relator be expressible within the calculus - it is quite possible, with this definition, to have a language for which the interpreter is not computable. Secondly, there is only one interpreter for each language (as 6.4(3) shows) although there may be various relator expressions which have this interpreter as their value. (Thus we would not say that someone is writing a new interpreter for LISP, but that he is writing a new program for the interpreter.) Finally, as the two examples which follow will show, the vast majority of "programming languages" associated with a calculus are of minimal interest.

Examples. Describe the languages on RW which have X and Y for their interpreters.

For X we have $X\{p\}:x=y \iff \langle p,x\rangle Xy$, that is, $X\{p\}:x=p$; thus X defines the language of constant functions, which maps each "program" p into $\bar{\bar{p}}$.

For Y, $Y\{p\}:x=y \iff \langle p,x\rangle Yy$, so that in this case $y=x$ regardless of p; $Y\{p\}=I$ for all p.

A reasonable minimum requirement to place on a language if it is to be "interesting" is that it be capable of defining every relator which is expressible in the calculus associated with it. I will define this property in terms of the interpreter for the language.

6.4(5) Definition. An interpreter M associated with a calculus on the base set S is *universal* if, for every relator A which can be defined by an expression in the calculus, there is a program p in S such that $M\{p\}=A$.

6.4(6) Corollary. There is a universal interpreter for RW.

Proof. We saw at the end of Section 6.1 that every relator definable in RW is represented by a program in the language of 6.1(4). The interpreter corresponding to the function Sem of 6.1(4) is therefore a universal interpreter for RW. □

This is an existence proof, which, by itself, does not guarantee that the universal interpreter can be expressed in RW. In Section 8.2 we shall see that the interpreter is in fact computable in RW.

6.5 Operations on Languages

In the previous section I have been discussing interpreters from the point of view of specifying semantics. Their normal use in computing practice is quite different: an interpreter is a device which enables us to run a program in one language on a system designed for another language. We write a program for an interpreter in the host language which defines a "virtual machine" on which programs in the new language can be run. Interpretation is thus a language transforming operation.

There is another, still more common, language operation, which may be given the generic name "translation". It has various specific forms: compilation, assembly, macro-expansion and so on (just as "interpretation" has the specific forms of simulation, emulation, microprogramming and so on). I have defined an interpreter to be a relator, rather than a program defining the relator; similarly, I will define a translator to be a relator mapping one language into another. In the definition, the source and object languages will be specified by their interpreters L and M rather than their semantic functions.

6.5(1) Definition. The relator R on the base set S is a translator from the language of L to the language of M if and only if

$$(\forall p)(\forall q)(pRq \implies L\{p\} = M\{q\}).$$

In practice the translator is always specified by a program, say r. This will commonly be in the object language, M, but in the case of a cross-compiler it will be in another language again - say the language of the interpreter N. Thus R=N{r}. If R is deterministic we have

$$N\{r\}:p = q \implies L\{p\} = M\{q\}$$

from which follows

6.5(2) Corollary. If r is a program in the language of N for a deterministic translator from L to M, then, for all p,

$$L\{p\} = M\{N\{r\}:p\}.$$

6. Programs

A computation involving the evaluation of $L\{p\}:x$ is actually performed as $M\{N\{r\}:p\}:x$, a form which displays the two-pass character of this computation. The first pass is to compute $N\{r\}:p$, which gives the translated program, q. In the second pass, $M\{q\}:x$ is computed, to give the result of $L\{p\}:x$.

As an example, let us take the compilation of Pascal for the (mythical) Dido computer. Here, the base set S must include not only character strings and the various data types that can be used in Pascal, but also a representation of Dido machine language instructions and the data types that are used by machine language programs; or if they are not present in S, the relational calculus on S which is being used must be extended to include them.

Then corresponding to the computer there is a relator D such that $D\{q\}$ gives the input-output relation defined by any Dido program q, and corresponding to the language Pascal there is a relator P such that $P\{p\}$ is the function defined by the Pascal program p. The relator R corresponding to the Pascal compiler must therefore satisfy

$$(\forall p)(\forall q)(pRq \Longrightarrow P\{p\}=D\{q\}).$$

If the machine language program for R is r, this reduces to $P\{p\}=D\{D\{r\}:p\}$.

The definitions of interpreter and translator which I have given may be used to derive the sequence of operations needed to bootstrap a language from one computer to another. The following example is adapted from Sanderson [24].

Example. The problem is to bootstrap a compiler from an Aeneas computer to a Dido, using only the Aeneas during the process. The relevant interpreters defining the various languages and computers are

P Pascal,

A Aeneas machine language,

D Dido machine language,

L an intermediate language.

It is assumed that the following programs are available: in addition to the normal Pascal compiler t_1 running on the Aeneas, there is a Pascal to intermediate language compiler t_2 written in Pascal, an intermediate language to Dido compiler t_3 running on the Dido, and a simulator e for the Dido running on the Aeneas. The equations satisfied by these programs are

$$t_1 - P\{p\} = A\{A\{t_1\}:p\} \quad (1)$$

$$t_2 - P\{p\} = L\{P\{t_2\}:p\} \quad (2)$$

$$t_3 - L\{p\} = D\{D\{t_3\}:p\} \quad (3)$$

$$s - D = A\{e\} \quad (4)$$

The Pascal compiler c running on the Dido must satisfy P{p}=D{D{c}:p}. Our method is to make successive substitutions using the equations (1) to (4) until we arrive at a result of this form. First, though, we need a little lemma:

$$\begin{aligned} P\{p\} &= L\{P\{t_2\}:p\} && \text{by (2)} \\ &= L\{(A\{A\{t_1\}:t_2\}):p\} && \text{by (1)} \\ &= L\{A\{t_4\}:p\} && (5) \end{aligned}$$

$$\text{where } t_4 = A\{t_1\}:t_2.$$

Notice that t_4 is the result of using t_1 to compile t_2; it is (as the form of (5) shows) a compiler from Pascal to intermediate language running on the Aeneas. The method used here is characteristic of the whole technique: any time an expression of the form A{a}:b occurs, where a and b are pre-existing programs, we replace it by a program c=A{a}:b. This corresponds to the fact that, since we have an Aeneas available, we may use it to evaluate c by running program a with b as data. Now

$$
\begin{aligned}
P\{p\} &= L\{P\{t_2\}:p\} && \text{by (2)} \\
&= L\{L\{A\{t_4\}:t_2\}:p\} && \text{by(5)} \\
&= L\{L\{t_5\}:p\} \\
&\qquad \text{where } t_5 = A\{t_4\}:t_2 \\
&= L\{D\{D\{t_3\}:t_5\}:p\} && \text{by (3)} \\
&= L\{D\{(A\{e\})\{t_3\}:t_5\}:p\} && \text{by (4)} \\
&= L\{D\{t_6\}:p\} \\
&\qquad \text{where } t_6 = (A\{e\})\{t_3\}:t_5 \\
&= D\{D\{t_3\}:(D\{t_6\}:p)\} && \text{by (3)} \\
&= D\{(D\{t_6\}\cdot D\{t_3\}):p\} \\
&= D\{D\{c\}:p\} && \text{(6)} \\
&\qquad \text{where } D\{c\} = D\{t_6\}\cdot D\{t_3\}.
\end{aligned}
$$

The entire bootstrapping process may now be summed up by taking the "where" clauses in this derivation one by one, starting with the lemma, and using 6.5(2) to explicate them.

(1) Use t_1 to compile t_2, giving t_4, a P to L compiler running in A.

(2) Use t_4 to compile t_2, giving t_5, a P to L compiler in L.

(3) Use t_3 with the Dido simulator e to compile t_5 giving t_6, a P to L compiler running on D.

(4) Form the composition of programs t_6 and t_3 to give c, the required compiler.

The result of this process is effectively a two pass compiler which will run on the Dido. The first pass translates Pascal into the intermediate language program and the second pass translates this into Dido machine language.

Chapter 7. ASSIGNMENT AND EFFICIENCY

So far, in this book, there has been no discussion of the most ubiquitous program construction of all, the assignment statement. Even if one agrees with Backus [1] that the use of assignment is the cause of many of our ills in computing, there can be no grounds for ignoring it.

Assignment can only be understood in relation to the store, where by "store" I mean the object whose changing states reflect the effects of the operations being performed. Assignments are made to variables held in store, and values of these variables retrieved from the store, so that the store provides the underlying mechanism for the implementation of assignment. In a hardware computer it is a complex of hardware devices, in a virtual computer it is a data structure in some programming language, and in RW it is a variable taking values in W - yet these differences are less significant than those which arise from the choice of a static versus a dynamic approach to data storage.

A conventional compiler strips away much of the information provided by the programmer, so that it is only present in the run-time store in an implicit form. In particular, variable identifiers disappear, and are represented at run time only by the locations in which data are held. Similarly, multi-dimensional arrays become linear sequences of memory locations, and, in some cases, no information is stored concerning the boundaries of rows and columns (although this information must be implicitly present in the compiled program, of course, to permit accessing of elements). This is a static system, since it assumes that the identifiers and structures remain unchanged during the execution of the program. At the other extreme is a fully dynamic system in which all the information given by the programmer is retained explicitly at run time.

In Section 5.1 I argued the case for using dynamic typing in a relational calculus when dealing with a mixture of types. In this chapter I shall take the argument to its logical conclusion by developing a dynamic programming language for an extension of RW. This dynamic character will be manifested internally in the system by the retention of the typing and structural information supplied by the programmer, and it will be manifested externally in the language by the absence of declarations. A declaration, after all, asserts that some property of an identifier will remain constant during part of the execution of the program. In a fully dynamic system, no such guarantee can be given.

The choice of this approach does not imply advocacy of the indiscriminate use of dynamically typed languages in practical programming. It is, as I said in Chapter 4, a matter of factoring out questions related to efficiency, so that they can be treated separately. In Section 7.3 I will discuss the relations between static and dynamic typing, and the semantics of declarations. That section, therefore, provides the link between our theory and the normal, semi-static languages.

One objective in setting up this programming language for RW is to provide a framework for the understanding of assignment. Another aim is to give an example which is more extended than Examples 6.1(3) and 6.1(4), showing how the specification of a language using denotational semantics works out with a relational calculus. However, I have no intention of defining a full scale programming language, and many essential features have been left out. In particular, there are no procedures, let alone coroutines or facilities for parallel operation.

There are two reasons for this. The first follows from the purpose behind this book, which is to demonstrate the feasibility of a relational theory of computing in general terms, rather than making extensive developments in particular areas. Now it is clear that relational theory is suitable for expressing parallelism. For example, the relator $(A \cup B)^n$ denotes a sequence of n applications each of which may involve either A or B, while the use of the do od operation allows us to have a more restricted parallelism. However, the incorporation of these facilities in a language, and, in particular, the design of the facilities for communication between the various components of a program, is a problem which still needs much study.

The second reason for restricting the language is that it is not at all clear that the best way to define the semantics of a large and complex language is by simply making more extensive use of the standard techniques of denotational semantics. The method of Marlin [16], which involves distinguishing various aspects of a language and then using models to specify them separately, offers one possible way of bringing more order into the language design and specification process.

7.1 The Store

At any point during a computation, the store consists of all the variables which exist at that point, with their values. Using the definition of the structured data type, table, given in 5.3(6), we shall represent the store for our language by the table $[\overline{id_1}:v_1,\ldots,\overline{id_n}:v_n]$, where $\overline{id_1},\ldots,\overline{id_n}$ are integers corresponding to the top level identifiers, and $v_1,\ldots,v_n$ are the values of the variables. ("Non-top-level" identifiers are field identifiers occurring within records.) Suppose, for example, at a certain point in a computation, the variables were n - an integer, value 15,

x - an <u>array</u> [1..3] <u>of</u> integer, values 0, -3, -5,

r - a record with fields done = false, j = 21
and lastj = 19.

Then the store would be

$[\overline{n}:15, \overline{x}:[1:0,2:-3,3:-5], \overline{r}:[\overline{done}:false, \overline{j}:21, \overline{lastj}:19]]$.

If the assignments

r.j := 29,
x[-6] := 0,
r := 10,

were applied in succession, the resulting store values would be

$[\overline{n}:15, \overline{x}:[1:0,2:-3,3:-5], \overline{r}:[\overline{done}:false, \overline{j}:29, \overline{lastj}:19]]$,

$[\overline{n}:15, \overline{x}:[1:0,2:-3,3:-5,-6:0], \overline{r}:[\overline{done}:false, \overline{j}:29, \overline{lastj}:19]]$,

$[\overline{n}:15, \overline{x}:[1:0,2:-3,3:-5,-6:0], \overline{r}:10]$.

The second assignment illustrates the dynamic nature of structures in the language - a new element with non-contiguous index is appended to the array x; in the third assignment, the type of r changes from record to integer.

The distinction between arrays and records is purely nominal in this language. The element selectors are specified in the program as integers in the former and identifiers in the latter, but by the time they reach the store they are all integers, and both structures have become tables. I am assuming that some standardized mapping of identifiers into integers is used, and also, that the user will not mix the two types of element selector in one structure. (Insofar as there is a blurring of the distinction between subscripts and field identifiers in the store so that information given by the programmer is lost, the language is not "fully dynamic".)

Our language will permit nesting of arrays, files and records within one another to any depth. The relators ACCESS and ASSIGN of 5.3(6) on the other hand, do not provide for nested tables, so that they must be extended.

7. Assignment and Efficiency

ACCESS takes an operand of the form <z,j>, where z is a table and j an element of type integer, and obtains the j-th element of z. If we are to access an element within a nest of tables, we will require, in place of j, a sequence of integers corresponding to the sequence of identifiers and subscript expressions in the denotation of the variable. In fact, the most convenient way to arrange this in RW is to translate the variable denotation into a file of integers; this is assumed to have been done in the definition which follows, and I shall refer to this file of integers from now on as the <u>selector file</u> of the variable.

7.1(1) <u>Definition</u>.

```
Get = (WHILE NOT Y.EOF DO
          <<X,Y.LOOK>.ACCESS, Y.READ.X>).X
```

Suppose at some stage during the application of Get, the operand is

$$<z, [m_1,\ldots,m_{j-1}|m_j,\ldots,m_n]>,$$

where $[m_1,\ldots,m_{j-1}|m_j,\ldots,m_n]$ is the selector file of the variable, and z is the sub-table of the original table that remains after successive subscripting by $m_1,\ldots,m_{j-1}$. Then Y·LOOK has the value m_j, so that <X,Y·LOOK>·ACCESS gives the component of z having m_j for its index, while Y·READ·X gives the file $[m_1,\ldots,m_j|m_{j+1},\ldots,m_n]$. When the end-of-file condition is reached, the final X of Get discards the selector file, leaving us with the required result.

The corresponding assignment operation is a good deal more complex, since it involves effectively taking the data structure apart, changing one component which may be deep within it, and then reconstructing it so that all components which do not contain the modified component are unchanged. Although it is possible to specify this operation entirely within the calculus RW of 2.2(4), we can make the task very much less burdensome by using recursion.

7. Assignment and Efficiency

Suppose the nested assignment operation, Put, takes an operand of the form <<z,s>,y> where

z - (accessed in the operand by the relator X•X) is the structure within which the assignment is to be performed;

s - (accessed by X•Y) is the selector file; and

y - (accessed by Y) is the value to be assigned into z.

Then <X•X, X•Y•LOOK>•ACCESS gives the top-level component of z which is affected by the operation, and X•Y•READ•X gives the file s with the read-write head moved one place right, so that

<<<X•X, X•Y•LOOK>•ACCESS, X•Y•READ•X>, Y>•Put

will perform the nested assignment within this top-level component. That is to say, if we are working at some specific level within the nested structure, and assume that Put is available, we may use it to perform the nested assignment one level below the level at which we are working. Thus the modified component may now be introduced at the current level by means of the ASSIGN relator of 5.3(6). This provides the core of the recursive definition.

7.1(2) <u>Definition</u>.

```
rec Put = IF X•Y•EOF
              THEN Y
              ELSE (<<X•X,X•Y•LOOK>,
                        <<<X•X,X•Y•LOOK>•ACCESS,X•Y•READ•X>,Y>•Put>
                                   •ASSIGN)
```

7.2 <u>The Assignment Language</u>

Any theory of computation in which all the information within the system at a given time is combined into a single state is bound to treat assignment as we have done in Section 7.1. The statement v:=e, from this point of view, represents an operator mapping one state into another.

In setting up an example of a language embodying assignment I shall follow Strachey's lead, and give only a skeleton syntax, which the reader may fill out and disambiguate according to taste.

7.2(1) Syntax.

Programs

```
        p ::= s
```

Statements

```
        s ::= dummy | v:=e | read(v,v) | look(v,v) | write(v,v)
              | rewind(v) | s;s | if e then s else s
              | while e do s
```

Expressions

```
        e ::= true | false | 'character' | number | newfile |
              newtable | v | eof(v) | [cl] | mop e | e dyop e
```

Component Lists

```
       cl ::= index: e | cl, index: e
```

Indices

```
    index ::= e | identifier
```

Monadic Operators

```
      mop ::= + | - | ~
```

Dyadic Operators

```
     dyop ::= < | ≤ | = | ≠ | ≥ | > | + | - | * | div | mod | ∧
              | ∨
```

Variables

```
        v ::= var
      var ::= identifier | var[e] | var·identifier
```

Much of the semantics of this language is entirely routine, and can safely be left out of this account. I shall concentrate on the parts which raise issues of interest, and simply sketch in the rest, starting with the most basic elements from the syntax for expressions.

$\text{Sem}[\![\underline{\text{true}}]\!] = \text{TRUE}$ (see 5.3(1))

$\text{Sem}[\![\underline{\text{false}}]\!] = \text{FALSE}$

$\text{Sem}[\![\text{'character'}]\!] = \langle \overline{\overline{\text{char}}}, \text{C(character)} \rangle$

$\text{Sem}[\![\text{number}]\!] = \langle\overline{\overline{\text{integer}}}, \langle N(\text{number}), \overline{\overline{0}}\rangle\rangle$

$\text{Sem}[\![\text{identifier}]\!] = \langle\overline{\overline{\text{integer}}}, \langle \text{Id}(\text{identifier}), \overline{\overline{0}}\rangle\rangle$

Sem[[<u>newfile</u>]] = NEWFILE (see 5.3(5))

Sem[[<u>newtable</u>]] = NEWTABLE (see 5.3(6))

In these equations, the functions C, N and Id each map their argument into the constant relator corresponding to an untyped numeral. If the code for the letter 'B' is 66_{10}, for example, we would have $C('B') = \overline{\overline{66}}$, and $\text{Sem}[\![B]\!] = \langle\overline{\overline{\text{char}}}, \overline{\overline{66}}\rangle$. Similarly, $N(12) = \overline{\overline{12}}$, and $\text{Sem}[\![12]\!] = \langle\overline{\overline{\text{integer}}}, \langle\overline{\overline{12}}, \overline{\overline{0}}\rangle\rangle$. Id is derived from the mapping of identifiers into integers which was mentioned in Section 7.1. The next alternative under "expressions" is v, so we will digress to look at the variables.

The syntax for variables makes use of an auxiliary equation, v::=var, to simplify the semantic description. (I shall change the style of presentation a little at this point, to avoid potential ambiguities. In a case like

var ::= identifier | var [e] | var·identifier

I shall state the alternatives one by one, inserting subscripts where necessary -

var ::= identifier

var_1 ::= var_2[e]

var_1 ::= var_2·identifier

and give the semantic equations below the alternatives.)

var ::= identifier

Sem[[var]] = <I,<NEWFILE, Sem[[identifier]]>·WRITE>.

The effect of <NEWFILE, Sem[[identifier]]>·WRITE is to give a file containing one element, the integer corresponding to the leading identifier of the variable - this is the selector file for a variable consisting of just this identifier. Thus the expression just given for Sem[[var]] yields the pair with the store as its first element and this file as its second. The other two alternatives will retain this pair format, while adding elements to the selector file.

Example. Suppose the leading identifier were 'q'. Then, corresponding to this we use the equation for Sem⟦identifier⟧ given earlier to get

Q_1 = <integer, <Id('q'),$\overline{0}$>>.

This is substituted in the equation above to form

Q_2 = <I, <NEWFILE, Q_1>•WRITE>.

Next, continuing with the semantics of variables, we have

var$_1$ ::= var$_2$[e]

Sem⟦var$_1$⟧ = Sem⟦var$_2$⟧•<X, <Y, X•Sem⟦e⟧>•WRITE>.

Sem⟦var$_2$⟧ results in a store-file pair, as I have explained. In <Y, X•Sem⟦e⟧>•WRITE the X yields the store, from which Sem⟦e⟧ computes the expression e; the effect of this is therefore to write this value on the end of the previous file, given by Y. <X, <Y, X•Sem⟦e⟧>.WRITE> produces a new store-file pair, with the updated file as the second component.

The third component is treated in the same way, with Sem⟦identifier⟧ replacing Sem⟦e⟧:

var$_1$ ::= var$_2$•identifier

Sem⟦var$_1$⟧ = Sem⟦var$_2$⟧•<X, <Y, X•Sem⟦identifier⟧>•WRITE>.

The value of Sem⟦var⟧ is a store-file pair, of which only the file (namely, the selector file) is needed; also, this file will be in end-of-file condition, whereas it will be required in rewound condition by the relators Get and Put. Thus we have the auxiliary equation,

v ::= var

Sem⟦v⟧ = Sem⟦var⟧•Y•REWIND.

Example. Following through the semantics of the variable 'q' from the previous example, we may now write

Q_3 = Q_2•Y•REWIND

for the semantics of this variable, or

Q_3 = <I,<NEWFILE,<integer,<Id('q'),$\overline{0}$>>>•WRITE>•Y•REWIND,

to give it its full value.

7. Assignment and Efficiency

We may now go back to the semantics of the expressions.

e ::= v

Sem⟦e⟧ = <I, Sem⟦v⟧>•Get

e ::= <u>eof</u>(v)

Sem⟦e⟧ = <I, Sem⟦v⟧>•Get•EOF.

Application of <I, Sem⟦v⟧> to the store yields a pair comprising the store and the selector file for variable v. Get selects v from the store; and in the case of <u>eof</u>, EOF then tests this.

<u>Example</u>. When the variable ′q′ occurs in an expression, the relator to access it is given by

Q_4 = <I, Q_3>•Get,

where Q_3 is the relator derived in the previous example.

The alternative [cl] under "expression" makes it possible to write a record or array into the program explicitly. For example,

y := [degree: 3, coeft: [0:1, 1:-3, 2:3, 3:1]]

would assign the record shown to y. Following this, the value of y•coeft[2] would be 3. The semantics of the component lists is given by

cl ::= index: e

Sem⟦cl⟧ = <I,<<NEWTABLE,Sem⟦index⟧>,Sem⟦e⟧>•ASSIGN>

cl_1 ::= cl_2, index: e

Sem⟦cl_1⟧ = Sem⟦cl_2⟧ •<X, <<Y, X•Sem⟦index⟧>, X•Sem⟦e⟧>
•ASSIGN.

The same device is used here as was used with the variables: a copy of the store is retained along with the table which is being constructed to allow evaluation of Sem⟦index⟧ and Sem⟦e⟧. Each index:e pair is inserted in the table as it is evaluated. The store is removed under the alternative in "expression":

e ::= [cl]

Sem⟦e⟧ = Sem⟦cl⟧ •Y

I will give only one instance of an expression involving an operator.

e_1 ::= e_2 dyop e_3

Sem[[e_1]] = <Sem[[e_2]],Sem[[e_3]]>·Sem[[dyop]]

dyop ::= -

Sem[[dyop]] = DIFF

Example. As a sequel to the previous examples, consider the expression 'q-2'. The semantic equations just given yield

Q_5 = <Sem[[q]], Sem[[2]]>·Sem[[-]]

= <Q_4, Sem[[2]]>·DIFF.

Let us now turn to the statements, and start by disposing of the cases where the semantics are obvious.

s ::= dummy

Sem[[s]] = I

s_1 ::= s_2;s_3

Sem[[s_1]] = Sem[[s_2]]·Sem[[s_3]]

s_1 ::= if e then s_2 else s_3

Sem[[s_1]] = IF Sem[[e]] THEN Sem[[s_2]] ELSE Sem[[s_3]]

s_1 ::= while e do s_2

Sem[[s_1]] = WHILE Sem[[e]] DO Sem[[s_2]].

The semantics of the assignment statement is given in terms of the relator Put.

s_2 ::= v:=e

Sem[[s]] = <<I, Sem[[v]]>, Sem[[e]]>·Put.

Example. As the last of the series of examples about 'q', take the assignment statement 'q:=q-2'. In the foregoing equation, Sem[[v]] refers to the relator which produces the selector file corresponding to 'q', that is, to the relator Q_3. Thus

Sem[[q:=q-2]] = <<I, Q_3>, Q_5>·Put.

The file operations have the most complex semantics of any in this language; I shall show how the semantics of read(v_1,v_2) may be derived. What is required is that the file f which is held in the store as v_1 have a read operation performed on it, so that the read-write head moves one place right, and that the value read from the file be assigned into the variable v_2.

Let

- s be the original store
- $f = [x_1,\ldots,x_{j-1}|x_j,\ldots,x_n]$ be the file stored in the variable v_1,
- $f' = [x_1,\ldots,x_j|x_{j+1},\ldots,x_n]$ be the file after a read has been performed,
- s′ be the store s with f′ assigned into v_1,
- s″ be the store s′ with x_j assigned into v_2.

The operation is achieved in four steps,

$$<I, <I,Sem[\![v_1]\!]>\cdot Get>:s = <s,f>,$$
$$<X, Y\cdot READ>:<s,f> = <s, <f',x_j>>,$$
$$<<X\cdot<I, Sem[\![v_1]\!]>, Y\cdot X>\cdot Put, Y\cdot Y>:<s, <f',x_j>> = <s', x_j>,$$
$$<X\cdot<I, Sem[\![v_2]\!]>, Y>\cdot Put:<s', x_j> = s''.$$

Combining these equations, we get

$s ::= \underline{read}(v_1, v_2)$

$$\begin{aligned} Sem[\![s]\!] = {} & <I, <I, Sem[\![v_1]\!]>\cdot Get> \\ & \cdot<X, Y\cdot READ> \\ & \cdot<<X\cdot<I, Sem[\![v_1]\!]>, Y\cdot X>\cdot Put, Y\cdot Y> \\ & \cdot<X\cdot<I, Sem[\![v_2]\!]>, Y>\cdot Put \end{aligned}$$

This expression may be simplified somewhat by using Theorem 3.4(4).

$$\begin{aligned} Sem[\![s]\!] = {} & <I, <I, Sem[\![v_1]\!]>\cdot Get\cdot READ> \\ & \cdot<<X\cdot<I, Sem[\![v_1]\!]>, Y\cdot X>\cdot Put\cdot<I, Sem[\![v_2]\!]>, Y\cdot Y> \\ & \cdot Put \end{aligned}$$

All the semantic equations in the section have assumed that the relators are operating on a pre-existing store. This store must be set up before the first statement in the program is executed, and must be discarded, to leave only relevant results, when execution concludes. These housekeeping operations are carried out by the semantics for "programs". First notice that if we apply

$$<<NEWTABLE, \overline{\overline{input}}>, I>\cdot ASSIGN$$
$$\cdot<<I, \overline{\overline{output}},>, NEWFILE>\cdot ASSIGN$$

to an operand x we get the initialized store [input: x, output: [|]]. If x is a file it may be accessed using the file operations of the language. For example, if the first statement of the program were "read(input,a)", the first element of the file x would be read and assigned into the variable a created by the execution of the statement. Similarly, the value of an expression e would be written to the output file by using "write(output,e)". At the end of the computation, the relator

<I, output>·ACCESS

has the effect of discarding everything except the output file. Thus, for the semantics of program we have

```
  p ::= s
     Sem[[p]] = <<NEWTABLE, input>, I>·ASSIGN
                ·<<I, output>, NEWFILE>·ASSIGN
                ·Sem[[s]]
                ·<I, output>·ACCESS
                  where Succ = <T,I>,...
```

The *where* clause at the end of this expression is used to attach all the "system" relators which have been defined in the previous chapters. In the cases where I have taken liberties with the notation of RW it is assumed that the correct notation would be used; for example, WHILE P DO A would be replaced, whenever it occurred, by While(P,A).

7.3 Efficiency and Declarations

The language definition technique illustrated in Section 7.2 will be of little practical use while it is restricted to dynamically typed languages. The great majority of applications call for static typing because of the gains in efficiency and compile-time checking that it makes possible. Thus we ask, Can this definitional technique be used for statically typed languages, in which variable types are specified by declarations?

7. Assignment and Efficiency

At first sight it may seem that if we start with a dynamically typed language and add declarations to it, the semantics of the language is unchanged for programs which are consistent with their declarations. The declaration specifies that certain variables will have a given type throughout the execution. But the semantics, which covers all possible type changes, includes the situation where the type does not change at all as a special case. Therefore, it seems, the only effect of adding declarations is to produce an abort in any case where a dynamically typed execution would result in a variable having, at any stage, a type other than that declared for it.

Unfortunately the situation is not as simple as this, as the following example will show. Suppose, in the language of 7.2(1), we have the statements

```
read(input, x);
x := x+i
```

The addition operation will test the types of x and i: if both are integer it will do integer addition, otherwise it will do real addition. Thus if i has an integer value, the operation performed will depend on whether the read interprets its input as a real or an integer.

Now suppose we add the declaration

<u>var</u> x: real; i: integer

(using the syntax of Pascal [13].) The effect will be that the compiler will introduce two automatic coercions. Let "coerce(e,t)" be the function which converts the value of the expression e to type t. Then to get the effect of adding the declaration, we would have to have as the corresponding dynamically typed program

```
read(input,x1);
x := coerce(x1, real);
x := x + coerce(i, real)
```

In this case, real addition is performed regardless of the data input by the read statement.

7. Assignment and Efficiency

When the only coercion involved is from integer to real it will often happen that the final result is the same, regardless of whether static or dynamic typing was used. However, it would not be difficult to devise other examples where significant differences would occur. Thus, if the technique of semantic specification is to be applicable to languages containing variable declarations, we need to devise some way of coping with automatic coercions. I will suggest one solution, while noting that there are others which are equally possible.

First of all, recall that in the dynamically typed system every variable carries its type along with its value. Using this fact, we may extend the data representation to include an "unspecified" element of each type; denote the unspecified real number by U_{real} and the unspecified integer by $U_{integer}$. Then

(1) we define the semantics of a declaration as assigning unspecified values of the appropriate types to the declared variables - for example, <u>var</u> x:real, i:integer would result in $x:=U_{real}$; $i:=U_{integer}$;

(2) we change the definition of ASSIGN (5.3(6)) so that it never changes the type of a variable: if possible it coerces the value being assigned to agree with the type of the variable, and otherwise it aborts the program.

The effect of this will be a dynamically typed language which behaves exactly as if it were statically typed, at least where coercions are concerned. An added advantage of this approach is that, if one wishes to include the ability to initialize variables in the variable declaration, all that is required is to assign the initial value to the variable instead of the unspecified value.

To sum up, it has been shown in this chapter that (1) using a relational calculus, we can define the semantics of a dynamically typed language which provides assignment into fairly complex nested structures along with the usual statement constructors; and (2) that there are no serious obstacles to adapting these semantics to give the semantics of the corresponding static language.

Chapter 8. METATHEORY

The relational approach to the theory of computation is relevant to metatheory no less than to the other areas of the subject. In this chapter we shall look at three applications, all relating to RW. Firstly, we shall show that RW, and also the extension of RW obtained by allowing recursive definitions, both define all the computable functions. Secondly, we shall define a universal interpreter within RW for the language of 6.1(4). And finally, we shall derive some of the standard computability results for RW.

8.1 Functions Computable in RW

As I pointed out in Section 6.1, the set of functions on a countably infinite set is not countable, while the set of finite strings, and *a fortiori* finite expressions, that can be formed from a finite or even countably infinite alphabet is countable. Thus any system which represents the functions by finite expressions must necessarily leave most of them unrepresented. We shall say that the functions and relators which can be expressed in a given relational calculus are *computable* in that calculus.

There is a long history of theories of computability, of course. Turing [31], Kleene [14], Church [6], Post [22], Markov [15] and others have all developed systems which are capable of defining a set of "computable" functions. In some cases the system gives functions on the non-negative integers and in others functions on the character strings, but it is a simple matter to define a one-one mapping between the integers and the character strings and so compare the functions. The fact that each system defines the same set of functions lends empirical support to the thesis that this unique set comprises precisely those functions which are algorithmically definable, and capable of evaluation on a computer using finite resources of space and time. Naturally, we will expect to find that RW defines this same set of functions.

Let Q be the set of recursive functions on the non-negative integers, R_1 the functions definable in RW, R_2 the functions definable in RW if recursion is permitted, and S the functions definable in the lambda calculus. Then we know that Q=S, and it is obvious that $R_1 \subseteq R_2$. Our procedure will be to show that $Q \subseteq R_1$ and $R_2 \subseteq S$ so that it will follow that $Q=R_1=R_2=S$. This leads to two conclusions: (1) RW defines precisely the computable functions, and (2) any functions which can be defined using recursion with RW can also be defined without recursion.

8.1(1) Theorem. The recursive functions are computable in RW.

Proof. We shall set up a representation of recursive function theory, regarded as a relational calculus, within RW. I shall follow the formulation of the theory given in Mendelson [18].

Recursive functions may be defined on a base set consisting of tuples of non-negative integers. That is, the base set is N*, where N is the set of non-negative integers. We shall represent these tuples as stacks of numerals, using Definitions 4.1(1) and 5.3(4). Since a recursive function always has a single integer as its value, the output of the relator corresponding to the function will be a stack of depth 1.

The primitive relators of recursive function theory are, firstly, the constant function which maps its argument into zero, secondly, the successor function, and thirdly, the projection functions U_i^n which select the i-th element of the n-tuple $\underline{\underline{\ }}\langle x_1,\ldots,x_n\rangle$. We implement these as follows:

$\overline{\overline{0}}$·Stack for the zero function,

TOP·Succ·Stack for the successor function, and

POP^{i-1}·TOP·Stack for the projection function U_i^n

where Stack = <NEWSTACK,I>·PUSH has the effect of transforming its operand into a stack of depth 1.

There are three relational operations, of which the first is substitution. The function $k:N^n \to N$ may be defined in terms of $g:N^m \to N$ and $h_1,\ldots,h_m:N^n \to N$ by

$$k(x_1,\ldots,x_n) = g(h_1(x_1,\ldots,x_n),\ldots,h_m(x_1,\ldots,x_n)).$$

Let the relators in RW corresponding to g and $h_1,\ldots,h_m$ be G and $H_1,\ldots,H_m$. Then the relator corresponding to k is K, where

$$K = \langle\ldots\langle\langle H_m,\ H_{m-1}\cdot TOP\rangle\cdot PUSH,\ H_{m-2}\cdot TOP\rangle\cdot PUSH,\ \ldots\ldots,\ H_1\cdot TOP\rangle\cdot PUSH\cdot G.$$

Each relator H_j·TOP obtains the numeral corresponding to the result of h_j; this is then pushed onto the stack having the result of H_m as its base. G is applied to the completed stack.

The second relational operation, recursion, enables a function $k:N^{n+1} \to N$ to be defined in terms of other functions $g:N^n \to N$ and $h:N^{n+2} \to N$ as follows:

$$k(0,x_1,\ldots,x_n) = g(x_1,\ldots,x_n),$$

$$k(y+1,x_1,\ldots,x_n) = h(y,k(y,x_1,\ldots,x_n),x_1,\ldots,x_n).$$

Once again, the corresponding relators will be G, H and K. The result is obtained by first applying G once and then repeatedly applying H to a composite operand involving the current value of y, the result of the previous application of H and the original operand stack $x_1,\ldots,x_n$. To ensure that all the information required is available we shall use a data structure of the form $\langle\langle k(j,x_1,\ldots,x_n),j\rangle,z\rangle$ throughout the computation, where z is the stack $x_0,\ldots,x_n$ with x_0 at the top. The relator

$$\langle\langle POP\cdot G,\overline{\overline{0}}\rangle,I\rangle$$

applied to z sets this up initially. We then need to apply

$$\langle\langle Y\cdot POP,X\cdot X\cdot TOP\rangle\cdot PUSH,X\cdot Y\rangle\cdot PUSH\cdot H$$

at each iteration to get the next value of $k(y,x_1,\ldots,x_n)$, so that

$$\langle\langle\langle\langle Y\cdot POP, X\cdot X\cdot TOP\rangle\cdot PUSH, X\cdot Y\rangle\cdot PUSH\cdot H, X\cdot Y\cdot Succ\rangle, Y\rangle$$

is required to get the next value of the complete data structure. This operation is iterated x_0 times, so that we finish up with

$$\begin{aligned} K = {} & \langle\langle POP\cdot G,\bar{\bar{0}}\rangle, I\rangle \\ & \cdot\langle\langle\langle\langle\langle Y\cdot POP, X\cdot X\cdot TOP\rangle\cdot PUSH, X\cdot Y\rangle\cdot PUSH\cdot H, \\ & \quad X\cdot Y\cdot Succ\rangle, Y\rangle, Y\cdot TOP\rangle\# \\ & \cdot X\cdot X. \end{aligned}$$

The remaining relational operation of recursive function theory is minimalization. This defines $k{:}N^n \rightarrow N$ in terms of $g{:}N^{n+1} \rightarrow N$. $k(x_1,\ldots,x_n)$ is the smallest value of y which makes $g(y,x_1,\ldots,x_n)=0$. To implement this in RW we set up a loop which evaluates $g(y,x_1,\ldots,x_n)$ for each y, y=0,1,2,..., until a zero is found. The relator is not applicable to any operand for which no zero exists.

$$\begin{aligned} K = {} & \langle I,\bar{\bar{0}}\rangle\cdot PUSH \\ & \cdot(G\cdot TOP\cdot Nonzero\ ?\ \langle POP, TOP\cdot Succ\rangle\cdot PUSH) \\ & \cdot TOP\cdot Stack \end{aligned}$$

□

8.1(2) <u>Theorem</u>. Any function computable in the calculus obtained by extending RW to allow recursive definitions is computable in the lambda calculus.

<u>Proof</u>. (I shall assume familiarity with the lambda calculus. Introductions to it may be found, for example, in Stoy [29] or Sanderson [23].)

The elements t and f of W are represented by $\mathbf{tt}=\lambda x\,\lambda y\,x$ and $\mathbf{ff}=\lambda x\,\lambda y\,y$ respectively, and the pair <a,b> by $\lambda u\,uab$. Since $\mathbf{tt}ab$ reduces to a, $(\lambda u\,uab)\mathbf{tt}$ also reduces to a; this provides the basis for the implementation of the selection relator X as $\lambda z\,z\mathbf{tt}$ (with Y, of course, being $\lambda z\,z\mathbf{ff}$). We implement

T by $\lambda u\, tt$,
F by $\lambda u\, ff$,
X by $\lambda z\, z tt$,
Y by $\lambda z\, z ff$,
<A,B> by $\lambda u\, uAB$,
A·B by $\lambda u\, B(Au)$,
P→A/B by $\lambda u\, (Pu)(Au)(Bu)$.

If we write P?A=Q, the recursion P?A=P→A·(P?A)/I becomes Q=P→A·Q/I, so that P?A is a fixed point of G = λQ(P→A·Q/I); that is, P?A = G(P?A). Thus we represent

P?A by Y_λ(λQ(P→A·Q/I)

where $Y_\lambda = \lambda a\, (\lambda y\, a(yy))(\lambda y\, a(yy))$.

If a recursion of the form x=A occurs in the expression being implemented, where A is a relational expression in x, it may again be eliminated by using Y_λ. □

The line of reasoning explained just before Theorem 8.1(1) now leads us to the two conclusions foreshadowed there.

8.1(3) Corollary. A function is computable in RW if and only if it is a recursive function.

8.1(4) Corollary. Any function that can be defined in RW with the addition of recursion can also be defined without recursion.

8.2 A Computable Universal Interpreter

We can take advantage of this last result to settle a question which was left open at the end of Section 6.4 much more easily than would otherwise be possible. We proved, in Corollary 6.4(6), the existence of a universal interpreter for RW, without actually constructing one. To do this entirely within RW is laborious, since it effectively involves simulating recursive procedure calling using only iteration. But now, on the basis of 8.1(4), we can construct a recursive relator, knowing that its existence implies the existence of an equivalent non-recursive one.

8.2(1) <u>Theorem</u>. The interpreter for the language of 6.1(4) is computable in RW.

<u>Proof</u>. The interpreter, M, is given by

<u>rec</u> M = <u>if</u>

$$\langle X\cdot X,\bar{\bar{0}}\rangle\cdot Eq \rightarrow$$

$$\underline{if}$$

$$\langle X\cdot Y,\bar{\bar{0}}\rangle\cdot Eq \rightarrow Y\cdot T \ \square$$

$$\langle X\cdot Y,\bar{\bar{1}}\rangle\cdot Eq \rightarrow Y\cdot F \ \square$$

$$\langle X\cdot Y,\bar{\bar{2}}\rangle\cdot Eq \rightarrow Y\cdot X \ \square$$

$$\langle X\cdot Y,\bar{\bar{3}}\rangle\cdot Eq \rightarrow Y\cdot Y \ \square$$

$$\underline{fi} \ \square$$

$$\langle X\cdot X,\bar{\bar{1}}\rangle\cdot Eq \rightarrow \langle X\cdot Y\cdot Y,\langle X\cdot Y\cdot X,Y\rangle\cdot M\rangle\cdot M \ \square$$

$$\langle X\cdot X,\bar{\bar{2}}\rangle\cdot Eq \rightarrow (\langle X\cdot Y\cdot X,Y\rangle\cdot M \rightarrow \langle X\cdot Y\cdot Y\cdot X,Y\rangle\cdot M \ / \langle X\cdot Y\cdot Y\cdot Y,Y\rangle\cdot M) \ \square$$

$$\langle X\cdot X,\bar{\bar{3}}\rangle\cdot Eq \rightarrow (\langle X\cdot Y\cdot X,Y\rangle\cdot M \ ? \ \langle X,\langle X\cdot Y\cdot Y,Y\rangle\cdot M\rangle)\cdot Y \ \square$$

$$\langle X\cdot X,\bar{\bar{4}}\rangle\cdot Eq \rightarrow \langle\langle X\cdot Y\cdot X,Y\rangle\cdot M,\langle X\cdot Y\cdot Y,Y\rangle\cdot M\rangle$$

<u>fi</u>

The structure of this expression corresponds exactly to the structure of the block of equations given in 6.1(4). I shall illustrate this for two of the equations, the third and the seventh.

We have, from 6.1(4), $Sem(\langle\bar{0},\bar{2}\rangle) = X$. According to 6.4(1) this means that we must have

$$M:\langle\langle\bar{0},\bar{2}\rangle,z\rangle = X:z.$$

Both $\langle X\cdot X,\bar{\bar{0}}\rangle\cdot Eq$ and $\langle X\cdot Y,\bar{\bar{2}}\rangle\cdot Eq$ yield t when applied to $\langle\langle\bar{0},\bar{2}\rangle,z\rangle$, so that the sixth line of the expression for M is relevant - $M:\langle\langle\bar{0},\bar{2}\rangle,z\rangle = Y\cdot X:\langle\langle\bar{0},\bar{2}\rangle,z\rangle = X:z$ as required.

The other equation from 6.1(4) is $Sem(\langle\bar{3},\langle p,a\rangle\rangle) = Sem(p)?Sem(a)$ so that, in this case we must have

$$M:\langle\langle\bar{3},\langle p,a\rangle\rangle,z\rangle = (Sem(p)?Sem(a)):z.$$

$\langle X\cdot X,\bar{3}\rangle\cdot Eq$ yields t when applied to $\langle\langle\bar{3},\langle p,a\rangle\rangle,z\rangle$, so that the second to last alternative of the main <u>if</u> <u>fi</u> of M is relevant. Thus we need to show that

$$(\langle X\cdot Y\cdot X,Y\rangle\cdot M \ ?\ \langle X,\langle X\cdot Y\cdot Y,Y\rangle\cdot M\rangle):\langle\langle\overline{3},\langle p,a\rangle\rangle,z\rangle$$
$$= (Sem(p)\ ?\ Sem(a)):z.$$

Now

$$\langle X\cdot Y\cdot X,Y\rangle\cdot M:\langle\langle\overline{3},\langle p,a\rangle\rangle,z\rangle = M:\langle p,z\rangle = Sem(p):z \text{ and}$$
$$\langle X,\langle X\cdot Y\cdot Y,Y\rangle\cdot M\rangle:\langle\langle\overline{3},\langle p,a\rangle\rangle,z\rangle$$
$$= \langle\langle\overline{3},\langle p,a\rangle\rangle,\ M:\langle a,z\rangle\rangle$$
$$= \langle\langle\overline{3},\langle p,a\rangle\rangle,\ Sem(a):z\rangle$$

so that $\langle X\cdot Y\cdot X,Y\rangle\cdot M\ ?\ \langle X,\langle X\cdot Y\cdot Y,Y\rangle\cdot M\rangle$ will have the effect of applying Sem(a) to the second component of $\langle\langle\overline{3},\langle p,a\rangle\rangle,z\rangle$ as long as Sem(p):z yields t. The final Y extracts the second component when the iteration is complete.

Notice, finally, that the guards in both the _if fi_ constructs are mutually exclusive total predicates so that, by 2.2(6), the use of these constructs does not take us outside RW.

□

8.3 Functions not Computable in RW

Since we know that there are bound to be functions which are not computable in any given relational calculus, there is interest in identifying some of these functions - the more so because it turns out that many of them would be very useful if only they were available. In this section I shall show how some of the well known results of computability theory may be derived for RW.

Throughout the section I will assume that M is a universal interpreter for a language on RW; the terms "program" and "language" will always refer to this language. Since M is universal, there must be a program for every function computable in RW.

Extending Definition 3.3(3), we say that P is a _total predicate_ if P is a function and $(\forall x)(P{:}x=t \vee P{:}x=f)$. Also, we say that the program p is _applicable_ to x if $(\exists y)\langle p,x\rangle My$, and that p is _self-applicable_ if $(\exists y)\langle p,p\rangle My$.

8.3(1) <u>Theorem</u>. There is no total predicate Q computable in RW such that, for all p in W, $Q{:}p=t$ if and only if p is self-applicable.

<u>Proof</u>. We assume that Q exists and demonstrate a contradiction. Since Q is a total predicate,

$$(\forall p)(pQf \iff \sim(\exists y)\langle p,p\rangle My).$$

Let $V=Q?I$, so that $(\forall p)((\exists y)pVy \iff pQf)$ by 3.3(3) - that is,

$$(\forall p)((\exists y)pVy \iff \sim(\exists y)\langle p,p\rangle My).$$

Let v be a program for V so that $\langle v,x\rangle My \iff xVy$. Then

$$(\forall p)((\exists y)\langle v,p\rangle My \iff \sim(\exists y)\langle p,p\rangle My);$$

but substituting v for p in this gives a contradiction. □

This theorem, by itself, is of no great practical importance. Although we do sometimes use a compiler to compile itself, there is no need for a program to test for self-applicability in this case and the other cases that occur are of no interest. However, the theorem may be used as a starting point in deriving more useful results.

8.3(2) <u>Theorem</u>. There is no total predicate Q computable in RW such that, for all p and x in W, $Q{:}\langle p,x\rangle=t$ if and only if p is applicable to x.

<u>Proof</u>. Assume that Q exists:

$$(\forall p)(\forall x)(\langle p,x\rangle Qt \iff (\exists y)\langle p,x\rangle My).$$

Let $V=\langle I,I\rangle\cdot Q$. Then

$$\begin{aligned} pVt &\iff p\langle I,I\rangle\cdot Q\,t \\ &\iff \langle p,p\rangle Qt \\ &\iff (\exists y)\langle p,p\rangle My. \end{aligned}$$

Thus V would provide a test for self-applicability, contrary to 8.3(1). □

The idea behind this proof is that if we had a way of testing for applicability of p to an arbitrary x we could use it for testing applicability of p to itself, so that a relator Q satisfying 8.3(2) would solve the problem of 8.3(1). The V in 8.3(2) has the effect of transforming the general applicability problem into a self-application problem. Similar techniques are used in the theorems which follow, but they will require us to make assumptions about the programming language in use that are not necessarily true.

In Examples 6.1(3) and 6.1(4) we encountered a program constructor, comp, which was a function of two variables. It had the property that

$$\mathrm{Sem}(\mathrm{comp}(a,b)) = \mathrm{Sem}(a)\cdot\mathrm{Sem}(b).$$

Corresponding to comp we can define a relator C such that $C{:}\langle a,b\rangle = \mathrm{comp}(a,b)$, and, to give the same equation for the interpreter M,

$$M\{C{:}\langle a,b\rangle\} = M\{a\}\cdot M\{b\}.$$

Although it is theoretically possible to have a language for which C is not computable in RW, this will never happen in practice since there would be no computable parser for such a language.

The second assumption is stronger: there must be a computable relator K which maps each element r of W into the program for the constant relator $\overline{\overline{r}}$ (see 1.1(4)). That is,

$$(\forall x)(\forall r)(M\{K{:}r\}{:}x = r).$$

I shall come back to K again at the end of this section. In the meantime we have

8.3(3) <u>Definition</u>. A <u>CK-language</u> is one for which computable relators C and K exist, satisfying

$$(\forall a)(\forall b)(M\{C{:}\langle a,b\rangle\} = M\{a\}\cdot M\{b\}) \text{ and}$$
$$(\forall r)M\{K{:}r\} = \overline{\overline{r}}.$$

8.3(4) <u>Theorem</u>. In a CK-language there is no computable total predicate Q such that Q:p=t if and only if the program p defines a relator applicable to

(i) every element of W; or

(ii) no element of W.

<u>Proof</u>.

(i) Assume that Q exists: Q tests for a total relator, so that

$$(\forall p)(pQt \iff (\forall x)(\exists y)(M\{p\}{:}x=y)).$$

Let $V = \langle K,I\rangle \cdot C \cdot Q$, and let k_r denote the program for the constant relator, $\bar{\bar{r}}$; $M\{k_r\}=\bar{\bar{r}}$.
Then

$$
\begin{aligned}
pVt &\iff p\langle K,I\rangle \cdot C \cdot Q\,t \\
&\iff \langle k_p,p\rangle\, C \cdot Q\,t && \text{by definition of K} \\
&\iff (C:\langle k_p,p\rangle)Qt \\
&\iff (\forall x)(\exists y)(M\{C:\langle k_p,p\rangle\}:x=y) && \text{by definition of Q} \\
&\iff (\forall x)(\exists y)(M\{k_p\}\cdot M\{p\}:x=y) && \text{by definition of C} \\
&\iff (\forall x)(\exists y)(M\{p\}:p=y) \\
&\iff (\exists y)\langle p,p\rangle My && \text{by A2.}
\end{aligned}
$$

This contradicts Theorem 8.3(1).

(ii) Q tests for the abort relator, Z. The assumption is that

$$(\forall p)(pQt \iff M\{p\}=Z).$$

Put V = <u>not</u> $\langle K,I\rangle \cdot C \cdot Q$ and proceed as for part (i). □

8.3(5) <u>Corollary</u>. In a CK-language, there is no computable total predicate Q such that $Q:\langle p,q\rangle=t$ if and only if $p \equiv q$ for arbitrary p and q.

<u>Proof</u>. If Q existed it could be used to test for a program defining Z, contrary to 8.3(4). □

8.3(6) <u>Theorem</u>. In a CK-language there is no computable total predicate Q_a for arbitrary a in W such that $Q_a:p=t$ if and only if $M\{p\}=\bar{\bar{a}}$.

<u>Proof</u>. If the theorem were false we would have

$$(\forall p)(pQ_a t \iff (\forall x)xM\{p\}a).$$

Let $V = \langle I, \bar{\bar{a}} \cdot K\rangle \cdot C \cdot Q_a$. Then

$$
\begin{aligned}
pVt &\iff \langle p,k_a\rangle\, C \cdot Q_a\, t \\
&\iff (C:\langle p,k_a\rangle)\, Q_a\, t \\
&\iff (\forall x)\, x\, M\{C:\langle p,k_a\rangle\}\, a \\
&\iff (\forall x)\, x\, M\{p\} \cdot M\{k_a\}\, a \\
&\iff (\forall x)(\exists y)(\langle p,x\rangle My \wedge y\,\bar{\bar{a}}\,a) \\
&\iff (\forall x)(\exists y)\langle p,x\rangle My
\end{aligned}
$$

since $y\,\bar{\bar{a}}\,a$ is always true. This is a contradiction, since V would solve part (i) of 8.3(4). □

8. Metatheory

To sum up these results in the conventional terminology of computability theory, we may say that the following questions concerning a CK-language are undecidable, with the first two being undecidable for a wider class of languages:

(1) whether a program is self-applicable,

(2) whether a program is applicable to a given datum,

(3) whether a program defines a total relator,

(4) whether a program defines the abort relator,

(5) whether two programs are equivalent, and

(6) whether a program defines a given constant relator.

The last result implies, in particular, that it is not decidable whether a predicate maps every element of W into t.

There is a curious ambiguity about those results which involve the relator K in their proof. If we look at an example of the way K works, it would have to take an element like <t,<f,t>> and analyse it in order to produce a program defining <T,<F,T>>. To perform this analysis one needs a relator which tests for equality of arbitrary elements of W, or, equivalently, a total predicate, Isatom, such that Isatom:x=t if and only if x is an atom. Now (I→T/T):x yields t if x is either t or f, but is undefined if x is a pair. Similarly, (X·F):x yields f if x is a pair, but is undefined if it is atomic. In RW^+ we can combine these two relators simply to give Isatom = I→T/T ∪ X·F, but there seems to be no way in which these or similar relators could be combined in RW to give a total predicate.

Although there appears to be no expression for Isatom in RW, we can set up a reproduction of RW in itself which does provide this relator. Represent t by <t,t>, f by <t,f>, and any pair <x,y> by <f,<x′,y′>> where x′ and y′ are the representations of x and y. Then we can implement T, F, X and Y and the four relational operations of RW. But, in addition, X implements Isatom.

Chapter 9. CONCLUSIONS

Since the aim of this book is to demonstrate the feasibility of the relational approach to computing, rather than to present a full-scale, ready-made theory, the unanswered questions and loose ends are at least as interesting as the positive achievements. In this final chapter I shall try to put both the questions and achievements in perspective.

First of all, our exploration of the mathematics of relators in Chapters 1 to 3 provided no surprises. Definitions and theorems were obtained without too much effort, and it seems that the work could be pushed much further in any direction that proved to be fruitful.

The various examples concerning the calculus RW provide a thread of continuity running through the book. In addition to their obvious purpose of illustrating the various points that are being made, they serve two purposes. Firstly, they show how the techniques we are discussing can be used to define *ab initio* a non-trivial language - the assignment language of 7.2. And secondly, they show how what I have called a "conceptual factorization" can be achieved in this definition. If one were to extract all the material involved in the definition, it would add up to a considerable bulk (especially if all the missing definitions which I have dismissed as "routine" were included). Yet, to a large extent, the components of this bulk are independent, so that the complexity of their sum is not much greater than the sum of their complexities - a desirable property.

The study of data types has several strands which must eventually be woven together in any comprehensive theory of computation. Because RW was needed for other reasons, I have chosen to follow up those strands which contribute to it, while neglecting others which do not. I have adapted the algebraic notion of a homomorphism to show how one calculus may be reproduced within another, and have used this technique to produce, firstly, an untyped implementation of the non-negative integers in RW, and then a series of typed implementations; and we have seen how the correctness of such implementations may be verified by reference to axiomatically defined abstract data types. On the other hand, there has been no attempt to exploit the parallels that exist between the ideas underlying relational data base theory and the present work.

I have made no attempt to formulate a relational treatment of approximation, but I believe that this is another area where development is possible. Scott's use of lattices [28] to deal with some aspects of approximation can be appropriated to our theory without having to import the whole apparatus of reflexive domains. Also, if Abst in Definition 4.1(1) is taken to be a relation rather than a function, some interesting possibilities are opened up in topics such as interval arithmetic.

The natural approach to programming languages in a relational theory is via their semantics (rather than their syntax, as has often been the case in the past); a program is a representation of a relator, so we move from the relator to the program. This view of things harmonizes well with denotational semantics, and I have devoted a good deal of space to showing how denotational semantics works out in our theory. In particular, the problem of proving the equivalence of two programs reduces to the problem of proving equality of relator expressions.

9. Conclusions

I have not dealt with axiomatic or operational semantics, since this would merely reproduce the work of Blikle [4]. However, it must be pointed out that Blikle's treatment of operational semantics is in fact but one application of what is potentially a much larger theory - I would call it the "theory of processors". We have defined a process in 1.5(1); a "processor" is simply a computational system within which a process can take place. Now once we have this concept of a processor, we are able to form links with a number of branches of computing science: automata theory (and hence formal languages), concurrent processes, Mazurkiewicz algorithms [17] to name a few; a digital computer is a processor, as might be expected, and so also, perhaps unexpectedly, is a formal theory in logic. The connection established in Section 5.4 between our relational theory and the formation of mathematical models should also enable results concerning processors to be applied to cyclical physical systems. In short, I would expect the theory of processors to be a major growth area in a relational theory of computation.

In Sections 6.4 and 6.5 I have given a formal treatment of a topic which is usually handled informally, namely the transformation of programs by means of interpreters and translators. One obvious possibility here would be to combine the idea of an interpreter with that of a processor mentioned above, thus recognizing the fact that an interpreter always involves an execution loop in practice. There may also be some interest in following up the idea that a translator results from loop optimization performed on this interpreter-processor.

Very little use has been made in this book of the fact that relator calculi lend themselves naturally to the description of concurrent processing. In fact, I stopped short the development of the language of Section 7.2 in order to avoid entering into a discussion of concurrency. Nevertheless, I believe that relational theory will eventually prove itself to be important in this area by providing a solid theoretical basis for the work that is now being done.

In Chapter 8 we have seen how some of the classical results concerning computability can be transported into relational theory. Other areas of metatheory can equally well be taken over. For example, the work of Chaitin [5] on complexity could be reformulated for RW by taking the complexity of an RW expression to be the number of nodes in its parse tree.

Appendix. RULES INVOLVING QUANTIFIERS

<u>Rules A1-A4.</u>

Let A be a predicate in x and D a predicate in which x does not occur free. Then

$$(\forall x)(A \wedge D) \Longleftrightarrow (\forall x)A \wedge D \qquad \text{A1}$$

$$(\exists x)(A \wedge D) \Longleftrightarrow (\exists x)A \wedge D \qquad \text{A2}$$

$$(\forall x)(A \vee D) \Longleftrightarrow (\forall x)A \vee D \qquad \text{A3}$$

$$(\exists x)(A \vee D) \Longleftrightarrow (\exists x)A \vee D \qquad \text{A4}$$

A typical use of these formulae in a proof might involve the step

$$(\exists w)(xAw \wedge wBz) \wedge zCy$$
$$\Longleftrightarrow (\exists w)(xAw \wedge wBz \wedge zCy)$$

This involves A2, and is justified by the fact that w does not occur free in zCy.

<u>Rule A5. Two Predicates with One Variable</u>

Let A and B be predicates in x. The table which follows associates a pair of integers with each of eight formulae involving A and B. Suppose M and M′ are two of these formulae, with associated pairs (i,j) and (i′,j′) respectively. Then $M \Longrightarrow M'$ if and only if $i \geq i'$ and $j \geq j'$.

<u>Examples.</u>

(i) $(\forall x)(A \vee B) \Longrightarrow (\exists x)(A \vee B)$ since the pairs are (1,0) and (0,0).

(ii) $(\forall x)A \wedge (\forall x)B \Longleftrightarrow (\forall x)(A \wedge B)$ since both have the pairs (2,2).

(iii) $(\forall x)A \vee (\forall x)B$ and $(\exists x)(A \wedge B)$ are unrelated, since the pairs are (2,0) and (0,2).

(i,j)	M
(2,2)	$(\forall x)A\wedge(\forall x)B$
(2,2)	$(\forall x)(A\wedge B)$
(2,0)	$(\forall x)A\vee(\forall x)B$
(1,0)	$(\forall x)(A\vee B)$
(0,2)	$(\exists x)(A\wedge B)$
(0,1)	$(\exists x)A\wedge(\exists x)B$
(0,0)	$(\exists x)(A\vee B)$
(0,0)	$(\exists x)A\vee(\exists x)B$

Rule A6. One Predicate with Two Variables

The same method is used for determining the implications as in A5. C is a predicate in x and y.

Examples.

(i) $(\forall x)(\forall y)C \Leftrightarrow (\forall y)(\forall x)C$

(ii) $(\forall y)(\exists x)C \Rightarrow (\exists y)(\exists x)C$

(i,j)	M
(2,2)	$(\forall x)(\forall y)C$
(2,2)	$(\forall y)(\forall x)C$
(2,0)	$(\exists x)(\forall y)C$
(1,0)	$(\forall y)(\exists x)C$
(0,2)	$(\exists y)(\forall x)C$
(0,1)	$(\forall x)(\exists y)C$
(0,0)	$(\exists y)(\exists x)C$
(0,0)	$(\exists x)(\exists y)C$

REFERENCES

1 Backus,J. Can programming be liberated from the von Neumann style? A functional style and its algebra of programs. Comm. ACM 21, 8(Aug. 1978), 613-641.

2 Blikle,A. An algebraic approach to mathematical theory of programs. CC PAS Report 119, Computation Centre, Polish Academy of Sciences, Warsaw, 1973.

3 Blikle,A. An extended approach to mathematical analysis of programs. CC PAS Report 169, Computation Centre, Polish Academy of Sciences, Warsaw, 1974.

4 Blikle,A. A comparative review of some program verification methods. In: Proc. 6th Symp. Math. Found. Comput. Sci., 1977 (J. Gruska, Ed.), Lecture Notes in Comput. Sci. 53, Springer, Berlin, 17-33.

5 Chaitin,G.J. Information-theoretic limitations of formal systems. J. ACM 21, 3(July 1974), 403-424.

6 Church,A. The Calculi of Lambda Conversion. Princeton, Second printing 1951.

7 Dijkstra,E.W. Guarded commands, non-determinacy and formal derivation of programs. Comm. ACM 18, 8(Aug. 1975), 453-457.

8 Dijkstra,E.W. A Discipline of Programming. Prentice-Hall, 1976.

9 Ehrich,H.-D. Algebraic semantics of type definitions and structured variables. In: Proc. Fundamentals of Computation Theory Conf., 1977 (M. Karpinski, Ed.), Lecture Notes in Comput. Sci. 56, Springer, Berlin, 84-97.

10 Guttag,J.V., Horowitz,E. and Musser,D.R. Abstract data types and software validation. Comm. ACM 21, 12(Dec. 1978), 1048-1064.

11 Hoare,C.A.R. An axiomatic basis for computer programming. Comm. ACM 12, 10(Oct. 1969), 576-583.

12 Hoare,C.A.R. An axiomatic definition of the programming language Pascal. Acta Informatica 2(1973), 335-355.

13 Jensen,K. and Wirth,N. PASCAL User Manual and Report. Lecture Notes in Comput. Sci. 18, Springer-Verlag, Berlin, 1974.

14 Kleene,S.C. General recursive functions of natural numbers. Math. Ann. 112(1936), 727-742.

15 Markov,A. The Theory of Algorithms. Trans. by J.J. Schorr-Kon for the National Science Foundation, Washington D.C., 1961.

16 Marlin,C.D. Coroutines: A Programming Methodology, a Language Design, and an Implementation. Ph.D. Thesis, Department of Computing Science, The University of Adelaide, Nov. 1979.

17 Mazurkiewicz,A. Iteratively computable relations. Bull. Acad. Polon. Sci., Ser. sci. math. astron. phys. 20(1972), 793-797.

18 Mendelson,E. Introduction to Mathematical Logic. D. van Nostrand, Princeton, 1964.

19 Milne,R. and Strachey,C. A Theory of Programming Language Semantics. Chapman and Hall, London, 1976.

20 Park,D. Fixedpoint induction and proofs of program properties. In: Machine Intelligence 5(Meltzer,B. and Michie,D. Eds.), pp. 59-78. Edinburgh University Press, Edinburgh, 1970.

21 Pawlak,Z. Stored program computers (in Polish). Algorytmy 5(1969), 5-19.

22 Post,E. Formal reductions of the general combinatorial decision problems. Amer. J. Math. 65(1943), 197-215.

23 Sanderson,J.G. The lambda calculus, lattice theory and reflexive domains. Mathematical Institute Lecture Notes, University of Oxford (1973); and Tech. Report 73-01, Department of Computing Science, The University of Adelaide.

24 Sanderson,J.G. A basis for a theory of programming languages. Aust. Comput. J. 1, 1(Nov. 1967),21-27.

25 Scott,D.S. and Strachey,C. Towards a mathematical semantics for computer languages. Technical Monograph PRG-6, Programming Research Group, University of Oxford (1971).

26 Scott,D.S. Continuous lattices. In: Toposes, Algebraic Geometry and Logic (F.W. Lawvere, Ed.), Springer-Verlag, Berlin (1972),97-136.

References

27 Scott,D.S. Data types as lattices. SIAM J. on Comput. 5(1976), 522-587.

28 Scott,D.S. The lattice of flow diagrams. Technical Monograph PRG-3, Programming Research Group, University of Oxford (1970).

29 Stoy,J.E. Denotational Semantics: the Scott-Strachey Approach to Programming Language Theory. MIT Press, Cambridge, Mass., 1977.

30 Tarski,A. On the calculus of relations. J. Symbolic Logic 6(1941), 73-89.

31 Turing,A.M. On computable numbers, with an application to the Entscheidungsproblem. Proc. London Math. Soc. 42(1935-37), 230-265; Correction Vol. 43(1937), 544-546.

32 Wadge,W.W. A complete natural deduction system for the relational calculus. Theory of Computation Report 5, University of Warwick.

LIST OF SYMBOLS

INDEX

Index

Index